TOSEL®

READING SERIES

BASIC

READING 3

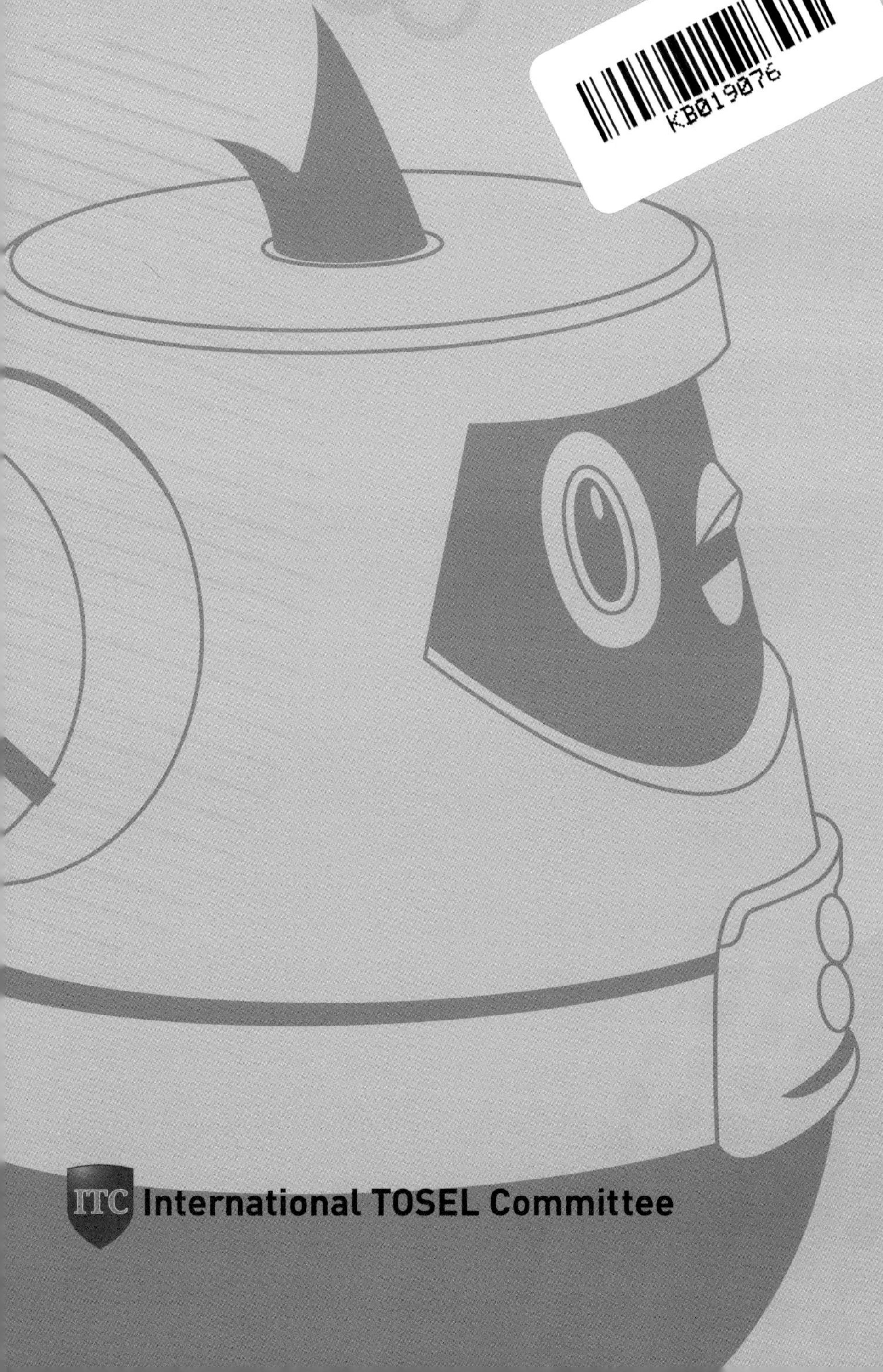

ITC International TOSEL Committee

CONTENTS

About TOSEL®

TOSEL (Test of Skills in the English Language) was developed to meet the demand for a more effective assessment of English as a foreign language for learners from specific cultural settings.

TOSEL evaluates and certifies the proficiency levels of English learners, from the age of 4 through adulthood, along with academic and job performance results.

Background

- Other English tests are ineffective in accurately measuring individual abilities
- Overuse of US-dominated testing systems in diverse cultural and educational contexts in the global English language learning market

Functions & Usage

- Assessment is categorized into 7 levels
- Used as a qualification for academic excellence for school admissions
- Used as a test to assess the English proficiency in the corporate and public sectors

Goals

- Create an effective tool for assessing and evaluating the English skills of English language learners
- Implement efficient and accessible testing systems and methods
- Provide constructive and developmental English education guidance

TOSEL® Strength

LEVELED ASSESSMENTS

An established English test system fit for seven different levels according to learners' cognitive development

ACCURATE DIAGNOSIS

A systematic and scientific diagnosis of learners' English proficiency

EXTENSIVE MATERIALS

Supplementary materials to help learners in an EFL environment to prepare for TOSEL and improve their proficiency

SUFFICIENT DATA

Content for each level developed by using data accumulated from more than 2,000,000 TOSEL test takers delegated at 15,000 schools and academies

CLASSIFIED AREAS OF INTELLIGENCE

Content designed to foster and expand the strengths of each student, categorized by the eight areas of intelligence

CONTINUITY

A complete course of English education ranging from kindergarten, elementary school, middle school, high schoool, and up to adults.

HIGH RELIABILITY

A high reliability level (Cronbach's alpha: .904 for elementary school students / .864 for university students) proven by several studies (Oxford University / Modern Language Journal)

SYSTEMATIC & EFFECTIVE ENGLISH EDUCATION

Accurate diagnosis and extensive materials which provide a step-by-step development in English learning, according to the quality of each learner's ability

TOSEL® Level Chart

Seven Separate Assessments

TOSEL divides the test into seven stages, by considering the test takers' cognitive levels, according to different ages. Unlike other assessments based on only one level, TOSEL includes separate assessments for preschool, elementary school, middle school, high school students, and for adults, which also includes both professionals and college students.

TOSEL's reporting system highlights the strengths and weaknesses of each test taker and suggests areas for further development.

COCOON

Suitable for children aged 4-6 (pre-schoolers)

The first step in the TOSEL system, the test is composed of colorful designs and interesting questions to interest young learners and to put them at ease.

Pre-STARTER

Suitable for children aged 7-8 (1st-2nd grades of elementary school)

Evaluates the ability to comprehend simple vocabulary, conversations, and sentences.

STARTER

Suitable for children aged 9-10 (3rd-4th grades of elementary school)

Evaluates the ability to comprehend short sentences and conversations related to everyday situations or topics.

BASIC

Suitable for children aged 11-12 (5th–6th grades of elementary school)

Evaluates the ability to communicate about personal information, daily activities, future plans, and past experiences in written and spoken language.

JUNIOR

Suitable for middle school students

Evaluates the ability to comprehend short paragraphs, practical texts, and speech covering general topics and to participate in simple daily conversations.

HIGH JUNIOR

Suitable for high school students

Evaluates the ability to use English fluently, accurately, and effectively on a wide range of social and academic subjects, as well as the ability to use sentences with a variety of complex structures.

ADVANCED

Suitable for university students and adults

Evaluates the ability to use practical English required for a job or work environment, as well as the ability to use and understand English at the university level.

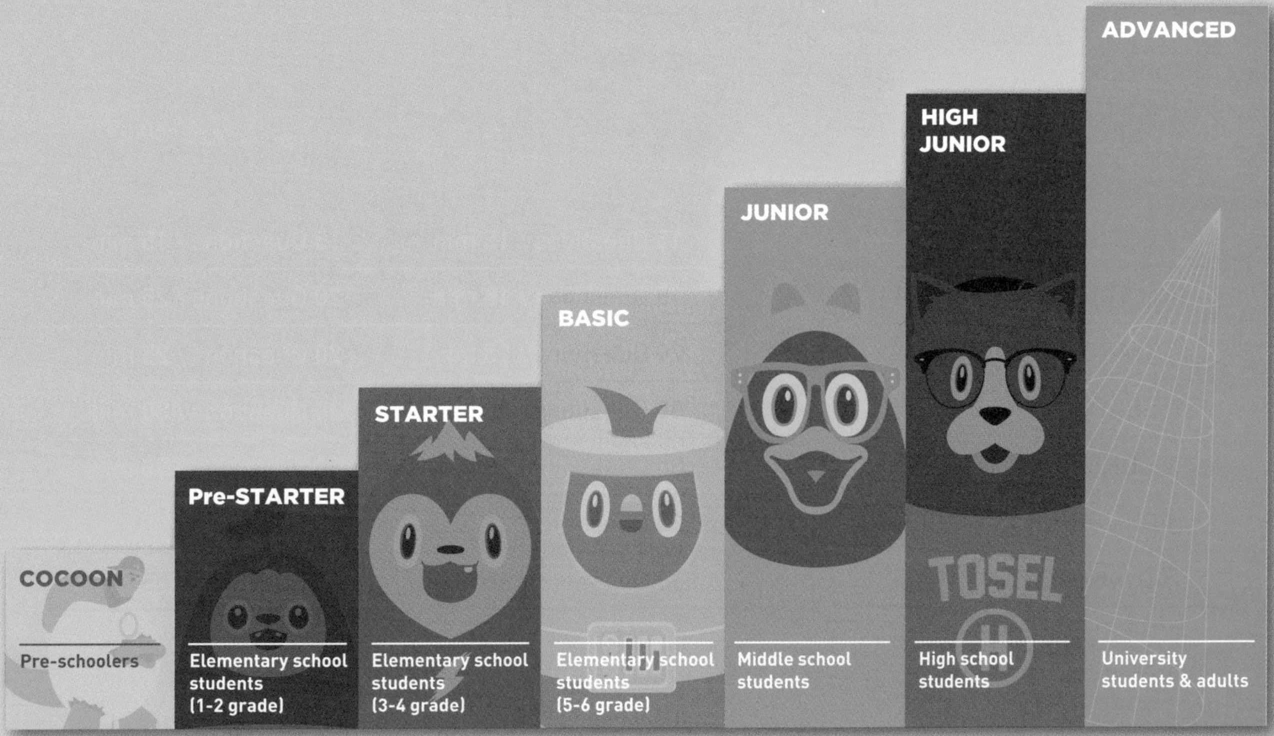

Evaluation

Assessing the Four Skills

TOSEL evaluates the four language skills: reading, listening, speaking and writing, through indirect and direct assessment items.

This system of evaluation is part of a concerted effort to break away from materials geared solely toward grammar and reading-oriented education.

TOSEL Test Information

Level	Score	Grade	Section I Listening & Speaking	Section II Reading & Writing
			Section	
COCOON	100		**15** Questions / **15** min	**15** Questions / **15** min
Pre-STARTER	100		**15** Questions / **15** min	**20** Questions / **25** min
STARTER	100		**20** Questions / **15** min	**20** Questions / **25** min
BASIC	100	1-10	**30** Questions / **20** min	**30** Questions / **30** min
JUNIOR	100		**30** Questions / **20** min	**30** Questions / **30** min
HIGH JUNIOR	100		**30** Questions / **25** min	**35** Questions / **35** min
ADVANCED	990		**70** Questions / **45** min	**70** Questions / **55** min

Certificates

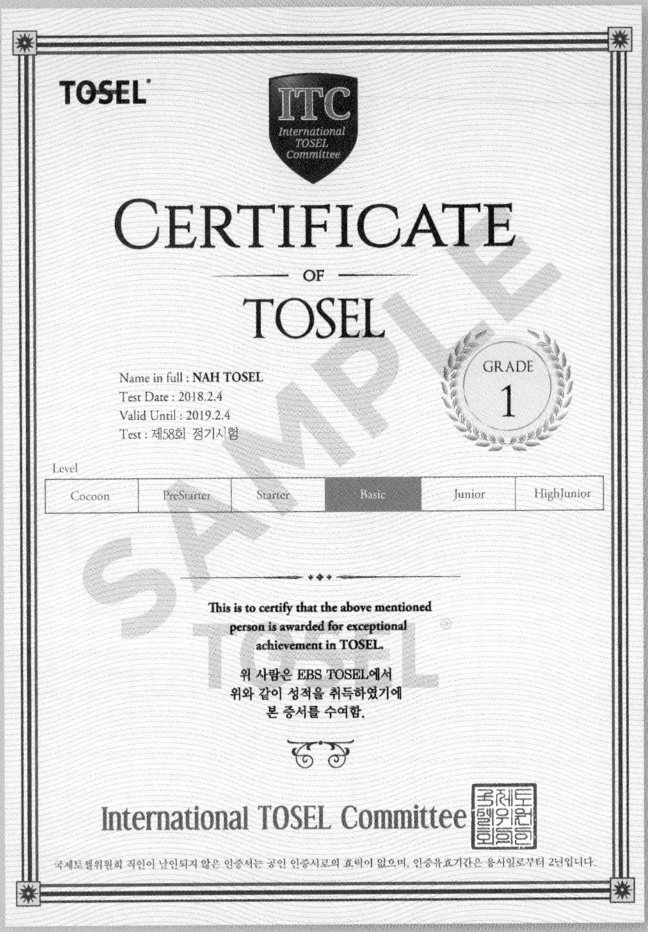
TOSEL

ITC International TOSEL Committee

CERTIFICATE OF TOSEL

Name in full : NAH TOSEL
Test Date : 2018.2.4
Valid Until : 2019.2.4
Test : 제58회 정기시험

GRADE 1

Level

Cocoon	PreStarter	Starter	Basic	Junior	HighJunior

This is to certify that the above mentioned person is awarded for exceptional achievement in TOSEL.

위 사람은 EBS TOSEL에서 위와 같이 성적을 취득하였기에 본 증서를 수여함.

International TOSEL Committee

국제토셀위원회 직인이 날인되지 않은 인증서는 공인 인증서로의 효력이 없으며, 인증유효기간은 응시일로부터 2년입니다.

SAMPLE

TOSEL Certificate

The International TOSEL Committee officially evaluates and certifies the level of English proficiency of English learners from the age of 4 to adults.

Certified by

Mar. 2010	Korea University
Dec. 2009	The Korean Society of Speech Science
Dec. 2009	The Korea Association of Foreign Language Education
Nov. 2009	The Applied Linguistics Association of Korea
Oct. 2009	The Pan Korea English Teachers Association

CHAPTER 1

Travel

Teacher's Book p.158

UNIT 1

Koh Lipe

What do you know about Thailand? Name three things.

UNIT 1 Koh Lipe

Do you want to enjoy the jungle and the beach at the same time? Do you want delicious food at a good price? Then you should visit Koh Lipe. Koh Lipe is an island in the south of Thailand. You have to take a boat from other islands to get there. I got to Koh Lipe by boat from Pak Bara.

So why is Koh Lipe so great? It is famous for white sand beaches and blue waters. The three main beaches are Sunset Beach, Sunrise Beach, and Pattaya Beach. I stood in the sand on the beach. I could see beautiful fish in the water. Also, on this island, people are very friendly. If you get lost, someone will help you. And the island has a special fire show. After the fire show, visitors can dance and enjoy wonderful food in restaurants.

Sadly, there are problems on Koh Lipe, too. The big hotels make a lot of garbage. And many people throw garbage on the ground. To solve some of the problems, now visitors must pay a fee to go on the island. The people on the island use the fees to take care of nature.

New Words

sand

n

ex Is it light brown and on a beach? It is sand!

sunrise

n the sun going up in the morning

sunset

n the sun going down in the evening

friendly

adj kind and open

visitor

n a traveler

fee

n money you pay to do something

10 minutes

Part A. Sentence Completion

1. We got to the island _______ boat.

(A) by
(B) for
(C) under
(D) around

2. There are _______ people in the room. It is crowded.

(A) as so
(B) so as
(C) too many
(D) many too

Part B. Situational Writing

3.

The island has a _______.

(A) tall building
(B) small pond
(C) high mountain
(D) beautiful beach

4.

They are _______ to each other.

(A) cold
(B) mean
(C) violent
(D) friendly

Part C. Practical Reading and Retelling

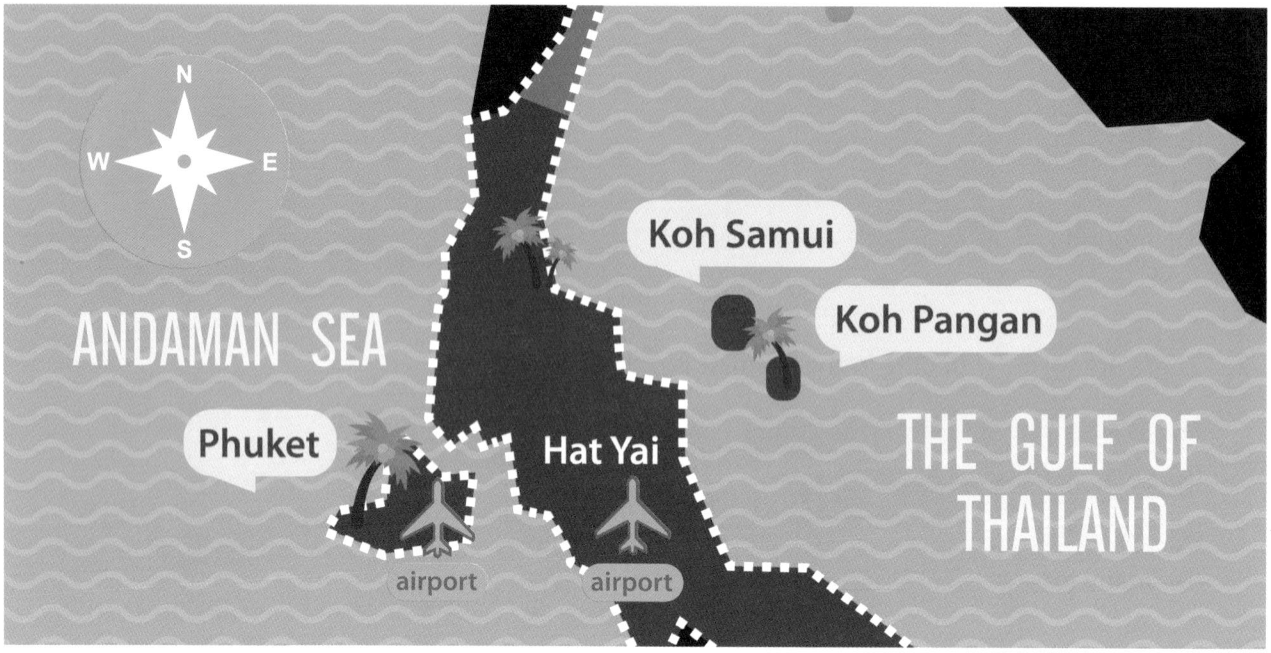

5. According to the map, what is true about Phuket?

   (A) It is an island.
   (B) It has no airport.
   (C) It is east of Koh Pangan.
   (D) It is between Koh Samui and Koh Pangan.

6. Where is Koh Samui?

   (A) west of Phuket
   (B) south of Phuket
   (C) near Koh Pangan
   (D) inside of Koh Pangan

Part D. General Reading and Retelling

Do you want to enjoy the jungle and the beach at the same time? Do you want delicious food at a good price? Then you should visit Koh Lipe. Koh Lipe is an island in the south of Thailand. You have to take a boat from other islands to get there. I got to Koh Lipe by boat from Pak Bara.

So why is Koh Lipe so great? It is famous for white sand beaches and blue waters. The three main beaches are Sunset Beach, Sunrise Beach, and Pattaya Beach. I stood in the sand on the beach. I could see beautiful fish in the water. Also, on this island, people are very friendly. If you get lost, someone will help you. And the island has a special fire show. After the fire show, visitors can dance and enjoy wonderful food in restaurants.

Sadly, there are problems on Koh Lipe, too. The big hotels make a lot of garbage. And many people throw garbage on the ground. To solve some of the problems, now visitors must pay a fee to go on the island. The people on the island use the fees to take care of nature.

7. What is the passage mainly about?

    (A) how to get to Thailand
    (B) the island of Koh Lipe
    (C) restaurants in Thailand
    (D) a nice hotel near Koh Lipe

8. What is NOT mentioned in the passage?

    (A) boat shops
    (B) beautiful fish
    (C) white sand beaches
    (D) dancing at restaurants

9. According to the passage, what is a problem of Koh Lipe?

    (A) The hotels are on fire.
    (B) There are too many fish.
    (C) People are hurting nature.
    (D) The boats are often broken.

10. According to the passage, how will Koh Lipe probably use the visitors' fee?

    (A) to make a new fire show
    (B) to get a boat to Pak Bara
    (C) to pay people to clean the island
    (D) to ask companies to build more hotels

Listening Practice

Listen and write.

MP3 B3-1

Koh Lipe

Do you want to enjoy the jungle and the beach at the same time? Do you want delicious food at a good price? Then you should visit Koh Lipe. Koh Lipe is an island in the south of Thailand. You have to take a boat from other islands to get there. I got to Koh Lipe by boat from Pak Bara.

So why is Koh Lipe so great? It is famous for white [1] ____________ beaches and blue waters. The three main beaches are [2] ____________ Beach, [3] ____________ Beach, and Pattaya Beach. I stood in the sand on the beach. I could see beautiful fish in the water. Also, on this island, people are very [4] ____________. If you get lost, someone will help you. And the island has a special fire show. After the fire show, [5] ____________ can dance and enjoy wonderful food in restaurants.

Sadly, there are problems on Koh Lipe, too. The big hotels make a lot of garbage. And many people throw garbage on the ground. To solve some of the problems, now visitors must pay a [6] ____________ to go on the island. The people on the island use the fees to take care of nature.

Word Bank

sand	Sunlise	visitors
send	Sunset	fee
bisitors	pea	frendly
Sunsset	friendly	Sunrise

Listen. Pause. Say each sentence.

MP3 B3-1G

Writing Practice

Write the words.

1 ____________ *n* ex Is it light brown and on a beach? It is ______! 	2 ____________ *n* the sun going up in the morning
3 ____________ *n* the sun going down in the evening	4 ____________ *adj* kind and open
5 ____________ *n* a traveler	6 ____________ *n* money you pay to do something

Write the words in each blank.

Summary

Koh Lipe is an ____________ in Thailand. It has white ____________ and blue water. The people there are friendly. Also, there is a special ____________ show. But the big ____________ and visitors leave too much garbage.

Word Puzzle

Complete the word puzzle.

1↓
the sun going up in the morning

2↓
kind and open

2→
money you pay to do something

3→
a traveler

4↓
Is it light brown and on a beach? It is ______!

4→
the sun going down in the evening

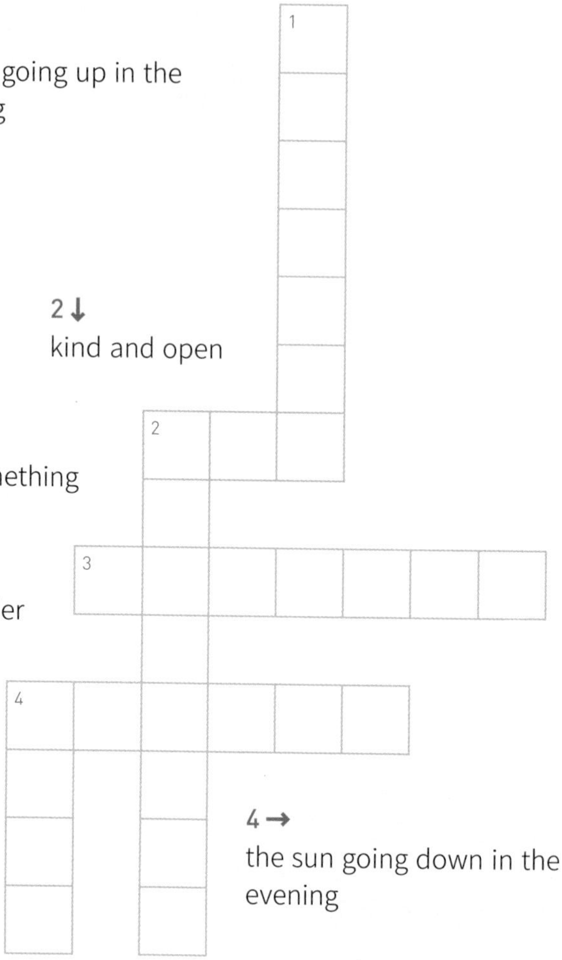

Teacher's Book p.162

UNIT 2

Flying to London

Imagine you have an airplane ticket. Where will you go?

UNIT 2 Flying to London

Anik's family is going to London on Tuesday. Anik's grandparents live there. Anik is very worried. He might get lost at the airport. And what should he do if he loses his ticket? He told his mom about his worries. Anik's mom laughed and told him all about the airport. Here are some things they talked about. On Tuesday, they are taking an international flight. That means they are leaving the country. First, they will check in. That means they will give their suitcases to some airline workers. Then, they will get their tickets. The workers will give them boarding passes. Boarding passes are tickets for airplanes. Then, Anik's family will get on the airplane. They will eat three meals there. After flying for ten hours, they will be in London. When they get off, they will go to the baggage claim area. There, they will get their suitcases back. Anik's mom said Anik's grandparents will be waiting outside. They will drive Anik and his family to their house. Now Anik knows what will happen. He is excited and not worried!

New Words

get lost
v not know the right way

all about
everything about

international flight
n an airplane ride to another country

suitcase
n a bag for travelling

baggage
n suitcases

baggage claim area
n a place in the airport to get suitcases

Part A. Sentence Completion

1. Nabi told Jason about his _______.

(A) worried
(B) worries
(C) to worry
(D) to worrying

2. My brother will be _______ for me outside the school.

(A) wait
(B) waiter
(C) waited
(D) waiting

Part B. Situational Writing

3.

My grandparents are _______.

(A) checking in quickly
(B) packing luggage at home
(C) driving us to their house
(D) standing outside in the snow

4.

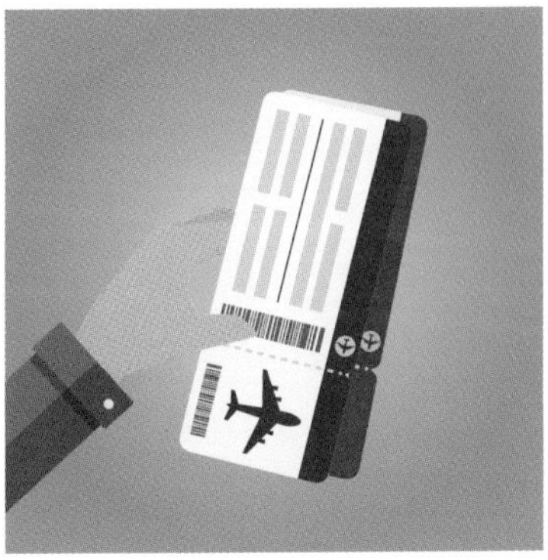

Brandon is holding a _______.

(A) airport worker
(B) shopping bag
(C) boarding pass
(D) large suitcase

5. When does the flight to Amsterdam leave?

(A) 20:20

(B) 21:15

(C) 21:40

(D) 21:55

6. Which gate is for the flight to Paris?

(A) 8

(B) 12

(C) SG 394

(D) HR 543

Part D. General Reading and Retelling

Anik's family is going to London on Tuesday. Anik's grandparents live there. Anik is very worried. He might get lost at the airport. And what should he do if he loses his ticket? He told his mom about his worries. Anik's mom laughed and told him all about the airport. Here are some things they talked about. On Tuesday, they are taking an international flight. That means they are leaving the country. First, they will check in. That means they will give their suitcases to some airline workers. Then, they will get their tickets. The workers will give them boarding passes. Boarding passes are tickets for airplanes. Then, Anik's family will get on the airplane. They will eat three meals there. After flying for ten hours, they will be in London. When they get off, they will go to the baggage claim area. There, they will get their suitcases back. Anik's mom said Anik's grandparents will be waiting outside. They will drive Anik and his family to their house. Now Anik knows what will happen. He is excited and not worried!

7. What is the best title for the passage?
   (A) Getting Lost in London
   (B) At the Airport to Shanghai
   (C) Mom talks about the Airport
   (D) Finding Grandparents at the airport

8. What will Anik do in the baggage claim area?
   (A) get on an airplane
   (B) buy airplane tickets
   (C) get his suitcase back
   (D) give workers his suitcases

9. What is NOT true about London?
   (A) Anik's grandparents live there.
   (B) Anik is going there on Tuesday.
   (C) Anik will take a train to get there.
   (D) Anik will take 10 hours to get there.

10. Which of the following will Anik do soon after he gets a boarding pass?
   (A) check in
   (B) go to the airport
   (C) get on the airplane
   (D) go to baggage claim

Listening Practice

Listen and write.

MP3 B3-2

Flying to London

Anik's family is going to London on Tuesday. Anik's grandparents live there. Anik is very worried. He might get [1] at the airport. And what should he do if he loses his ticket? He told his mom about his worries. Anik's mom laughed and told him [2] the airport. Here are some things they talked about. On Tuesday, they are taking an [3] flight. That means they are leaving the country. First, they will check in. That means they will give their [4] to some airline workers. Then, they will get their tickets. The workers will give them boarding passes. Boarding passes are tickets for airplanes. Then, Anik's family will get on the airplane. They will eat three meals there. After flying for ten hours, they will be in London. When they get off, they will go to the [5] [6] area. There, they will get their suitcases back. Anik's mom said Anik's grandparents will be waiting outside. They will drive Anik and his family to their house. Now Anik knows what will happen. He is excited and not worried!

Word Bank

sootcases	lost	all about
baggage	internationel	suitcases
allabout	claim	lest
clame	international	bagage

Listen. Pause. Say each sentence.

MP3 B3-2G

Writing Practice

Write the words.

1 ____________ *v* not know the right way	2 ____________ everything about
3 ____________ *n* an airplane ride to another country	4 ____________ *n* a bag for travelling 
5 ____________ *n* suitcases	6 ____________ *n* a place in the airport to get suitcases 

Write the words in each blank.

Summary

Anik and his family are going to ____________. Anik's ____________ live there. Anik was worried about going to the ____________. But Anik's ____________ explained about the airport. Now Anik feels better.

Word Puzzle

Complete the word puzzle.

1↓
a bag for travelling

2↓
an airplane ride to another country

3↓
everything about

4↓
suitcases

4→
a place in the airport to get suitcases

5↓
not know the right way

Teacher's Book p.166

UNIT 3

Petronas Towers

Is there a famous building near you? What is it?

UNIT 3 Petronas Towers

There are lots of great buildings around the world. Some of them are very famous, like the Eiffel Tower in France. There are some special buildings in Malaysia, too. They are called the Petronas Towers. The Petronas Towers are the main offices for an oil company called Petronas. They were the tallest buildings in the world until 2004. Now, they are the tallest twin towers. In 1992, César Pelli designed the Petronas Towers. The towers have a special design. The design shows Malaysian culture to visitors. Also, this building is very famous for a special bridge. There is a bridge between the two buildings. It is called the Skybridge. The Skybridge connects the 41st and 42nd floors of the Petronas Towers. For safety, only a thousand people can visit the bridge every day. That's why it is very hard to get tickets. Sometimes, people start to get in line from 6:30 AM in the morning. The Petronas Towers are not the tallest buildings in the world now. But they are still really interesting buildings to visit!

New Words

office *n* a business place	design *n* a pattern
twin towers *n* two matching towers 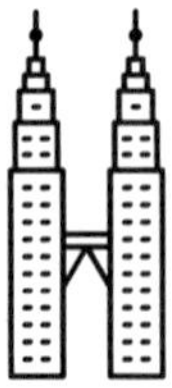	thousand *n* 1,000
safety *n* no danger	that's why it's the reason

10 minutes

Part A. Sentence Completion

1. Burj Khalifa is _______ building in the world.

(A) tall
(B) tallest
(C) the taller
(D) the tallest

2. _______ design is so pretty!

(A) This
(B) These
(C) Those
(D) That's

Part B. Situational Writing

3.

The team is _______.

(A) painting houses
(B) choosing clothing
(C) taking an elevator
(D) designing buildings

4.

There is a _______ between the two towns.

(A) truck
(B) bridge
(C) factory
(D) windmill

The Petronas Towers have shapes from Islamic culture.

Look at each tower from the top.
It is in the shape of a star.

Want to hear more about the towers?
Visit our website,
www.factsaboutthepetronastowers.web!

5. What shape is each tower from the top?

(A) star
(B) circle
(C) heart
(D) square

6. According to the ad, how can you learn more about the Petronas Towers?

(A) call them
(B) email them
(C) visit a website
(D) talk to a worker at the towers

Part D. General Reading and Retelling

There are lots of great buildings around the world. Some of them are very famous, like the Eiffel Tower in France. There are some special buildings in Malaysia, too. They are called the Petronas Towers. The Petronas Towers are the main offices for an oil company called Petronas. They were the tallest buildings in the world until 2004. Now, they are the tallest twin towers. In 1992, César Pelli designed the Petronas Towers. The towers have a special design. The design shows Malaysian culture to visitors. Also, this building is very famous for a special bridge. There is a bridge between the two buildings. It is called the Skybridge. The Skybridge connects the 41st and 42nd floors of the Petronas Towers. For safety, only a thousand people can visit the bridge every day. That's why it is very hard to get tickets. Sometimes, people start to get in line from 6:30 AM in the morning. The Petronas Towers are not the tallest buildings in the world now. But they are still really interesting buildings to visit!

7. What is the passage mainly about?
   - (A) the tallest building in France
   - (B) some famous towers in Malaysia
   - (C) safety problems of a famous building
   - (D) how to buy tickets for towers in Malaysia

8. According to the passage, how many people can visit the bridge per day?
   - (A) 1,000
   - (B) 1,992
   - (C) 2,004
   - (D) 3,000

9. What is true about the Petronas Towers?
   - (A) They are in France.
   - (B) There is only one tower.
   - (C) They have a special bridge.
   - (D) They are the tallest buildings now.

10. Why do people probably line up for tickets from 6:30 AM?
    - (A) The programs start at 7:00 AM.
    - (B) Many people want to visit the towers.
    - (C) The tickets are cheaper in the mornings.
    - (D) The Petronas Towers are closed in the afternoon.

Listening Practice

Listen and write.

MP3 B3-3

Petronas Towers

There are lots of great buildings around the world. Some of them are very famous, like the Eiffel Tower in France. There are some special buildings in Malaysia, too. They are called the Petronas Towers. The Petronas Towers are the main [1] ____________ for an oil company called Petronas. They were the tallest buildings in the world until 2004. Now, they are the tallest twin [2] ____________. In 1992, César Pelli designed the Petronas Towers. The towers have a special [3] ____________. The design shows Malaysian culture to visitors. Also, this building is very famous for a special bridge. There is a bridge between the two buildings. It is called the Skybridge. The Skybridge connects the 41st and 42nd floors of the Petronas Towers. For [4] ____________, only a [5] ____________ people can visit the bridge every day. [6] ____________ why it is very hard to get tickets. Sometimes, people start to get in line from 6:30 AM in the morning. The Petronas Towers are not the tallest buildings in the world now. But they are still really interesting buildings to visit!

Word Bank

That's	ofices	Thats
design	safty	safety
thousand	tovers	towers
offices	dezin	thausand

Listen. Pause. Say each sentence.

MP3 B3-3G

Writing Practice

Write the words.

1 ____________

n a business place

2 ____________

n a pattern

3 ____________

n two matching towers

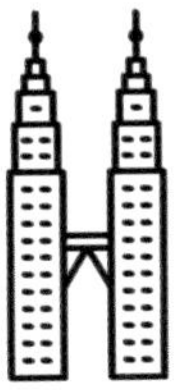

4 ____________

n 1,000

5 ____________

n no danger

6 ____________

it's the reason

Write the words in each blank.

Summary

The Petronas Towers are special ____________. They are the world's tallest ____________ towers. They have a special Malaysian ____________. A ____________ connects the buildings.

Word Puzzle

Complete the word puzzle.

1↓
1,000

2↓
no danger

3↓
it's the reason

4↓
a pattern

5→
two matching towers

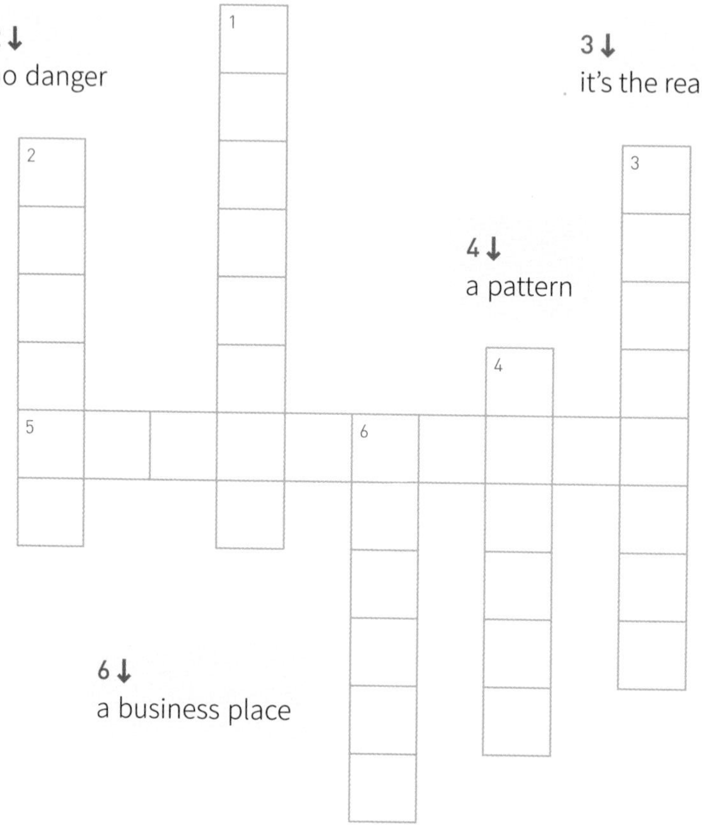

6↓
a business place

Teacher's Book
p.170

UNIT 4

Travel Manners

Think! You are traveling abroad.
Where are you? What rules must you follow?

UNIT 4 Travel Manners

Traveling is often very exciting. But if you remember some rules, it is even better! With no rules, you can make mistakes. Before you travel, you need to know good manners. So here is some advice for travelers. First, learn about the country. Learn its history, language, and culture. It will be fun! For example, in some countries, you can point with your finger. In other countries, that is not okay. Second, read the signs. When it says, "No Swimming," do not swim. It could be very dangerous or dirty. There is a reason for the signs. Third, watch and follow what others do. In many countries, you should not eat with your left hand. This is true in India, for example. So watch people when you eat at a restaurant, and follow what they do! Copying is the easiest way to learn. Finally, be careful when you take pictures. Taking pictures is fun in another country, but some people who live there might not like it. Also, museums and art galleries may not allow picture taking. Ask people before taking pictures. Remember these tips, and have a great trip!

New Words

travel *v* go on a trip	make a mistake *v* do something wrong
manners *n* ways of acting around other people	history *n* the story of a place and people
allow X *v* say X is okay to do	copy X *v* act like X

10 minutes

Part A. Sentence Completion

1. You _______ the artworks in the gallery.

(A) should touch not
(B) not should touch
(C) should not touch
(D) touch should not

2. Before Jim traveled to Haiti, he learned about _______ rules.

(A) it
(B) its
(C) he
(D) him

Part B. Situational Writing

3.

The sign says, "_______".

(A) No Running
(B) Please Run
(C) No Walking
(D) Please Swim

4.

For safety, the man should _______.

(A) walk faster
(B) stop walking
(C) jump into the hole
(D) look at his cell phone

Part C. **Practical Reading and Retelling**

Know Good Manners

Artist: Kid Cool

1
Don't forget to cover your mouth.
When you sneeze around others.
Use a tissue. Then wash your hands.
Around kids, fathers, and mothers.

2
Say the magic words.
Use them here and there.
Thank you, sorry, excuse me, please,
Are words for everywhere.

3
Be nice to others.
Stand in line and wait.
Don't throw trash on the ground.
That will make others feel great!

5. Which of "magic words" are NOT mentioned?

(A) sorry
(B) please
(C) excuse me
(D) you're welcome

6. According to the song, what should you do after sneezing?

(A) put on a mask
(B) save your tissue
(C) wash your hands
(D) cover your mouth

Part D. General Reading and Retelling

Traveling is often very exciting. But if you remember some rules, it is even better! With no rules, you can make mistakes. Before you travel, you need to know good manners. So here is some advice for travelers. First, learn about the country. Learn its history, language, and culture. It will be fun! For example, in some countries, you can point with your finger. In other countries, that is not okay. Second, read the signs. When it says, "No Swimming," do not swim. It could be very dangerous or dirty. There is a reason for the signs. Third, watch and follow what others do. In many countries, you should not eat with your left hand. This is true in India, for example. So watch people when you eat at a restaurant, and follow what they do! Copying is the easiest way to learn. Finally, be careful when you take pictures. Taking pictures is fun in another country, but some people who live there might not like it. Also, museums and art galleries may not allow picture taking. Ask people before taking pictures. Remember these tips, and have a great trip!

7. What is the purpose of the passage?
   (A) to explain stop signs
   (B) to warn about dirty water
   (C) to give advice to travelers
   (D) to teach readers how to swim

8. According to the passage, what is true about pointing with your finger?
   (A) It is bad in every country.
   (B) It is okay only in big cities.
   (C) It is bad in most countries.
   (D) It is okay in some countries.

9. According to the passage, what should you NOT do in India?
   (A) swim in a river
   (B) go to a restaurant
   (C) wear a hat outside
   (D) eat with your left hand

10. According to the passage, what should you do before taking pictures?
   (A) ask people
   (B) pay for pictures
   (C) hide the camera
   (D) raise your hands

Listening Practice

Listen and write.

MP3 B3-4

Travel Manners

Traveling is often very exciting. But if you remember some rules, it is even better! With no rules, you can make [1] ________ . Before you [2] ________ , you need to know good [3] ________ . So here is some advice for travelers. First, learn about the country. Learn its [4] ________ , language, and culture. It will be fun! For example, in some countries, you can point with your finger. In other countries, that is not okay. Second, read the signs. When it says, "No Swimming," do not swim. It could be very dangerous or dirty. There is a reason for the signs. Third, watch and follow what others do. In many countries, you should not eat with your left hand. This is true in India, for example. So watch people when you eat at a restaurant, and follow what they do! [5] ________ is the easiest way to learn. Finally, be careful when you take pictures. Taking pictures is fun in another country, but some people who live there might not like it. Also, museums and art galleries may not [6] ________ picture taking. Ask people before taking pictures. Remember these tips, and have a great trip!

Word Bank

maner	travel	manners
histry	allew	mistakes
mustakes	trabel	Coffeeing
allow	history	Copying

Listen. Pause. Say each sentence.

MP3 B3-4G

Writing Practice

Write the words.

1 ____________ *v* go on a trip	2 ____________ *v* do something wrong
3 ____________ *n* ways of acting around other people	4 ____________ *n* the story of a place and people
5 ____________ X *v* say X is okay to do	6 ____________ X *v* act like X

Write the words in each blank.

Summary

Remember these good travel ____________. First, learn about the country. Second, ____________ the signs. Third, ____________ others. Finally, be careful taking ____________.

Word Puzzle

Complete the word puzzle.

1 ↓
the story of a place and people

2 →
do something wrong

3 →
go on a trip

4 →
ways of acting
around other people

5 ↓
say X is okay to do

6 →
act like X

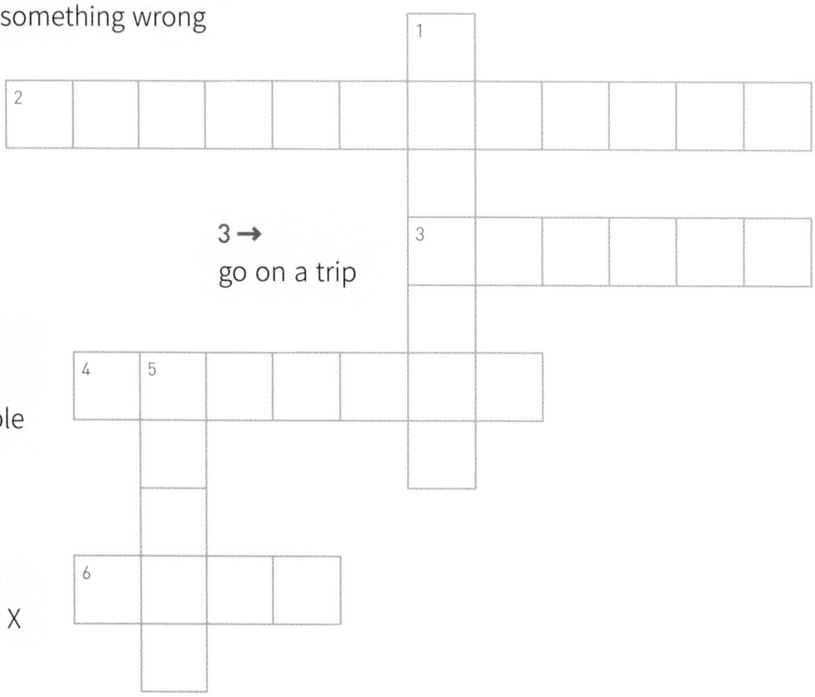

What Am I

Teacher's Book p.175

Read the passage.

Count: In how many sentences can you guess what it is?

What is this thing? It can be hard or soft. It can be in the shape of a square or a rectangle. It is not made of paper. It is not made of wood. You can take it on the bus or train. It has a handle, and maybe it has wheels. You can take it on a trip. You collect it at the baggage claim at the airport. It has things inside it. What is inside this thing? There are probably clothes in it. And there is probably a toothbrush and toothpaste. Maybe there is a pair of sunglasses. And if you are going to a beach, there is a swimsuit in it. If you are going to another country, put a book in it, too! A book of manners is helpful. So what is this thing? Now it's time for you to guess!

Now guess! What is it?

CHAPTER 2

Culture

Teacher's Book p.176

UNIT 5

Thanksgiving in Detroit

Your family is together for a holiday.
What is the holiday? What will your family do?

UNIT 5 Thanksgiving in Detroit

My mom, dad, and I live in New York. But my grandparents, aunts, uncles, and cousins live in Detroit. Every Thanksgiving, we travel to Detroit. My dad drives us to Detroit. It takes about 10 hours. When we get to Grandma and Grandpa's house, the adults start cooking food. My mom cooks turkey and sweet potatoes. My aunts make cornbread and apple pies. Grandma washes the dishes. My dad makes tofu salad and fruit dishes. Those dishes are for the vegetarians in the family. Vegetarians don't eat meat. Grandma is a vegetarian.

While the adults cook, the kids stay in the living room. We are all very close to one another. We play board games and card games. I like card games more because I always win. This year, my cousin Amy brought video games. So we took turns playing them. My cousin James won every game! After three hours, Grandma said, "Dinner is ready!" So we all went to the dining room and sat down to eat. There was a lot of food, but we ate it all! After dinner, we watched TV in the living room. We watched a parade on TV. It was very fun. Then we went to sleep. We have to drive back to New York tomorrow!

New Words

adult

n not a baby or child

turkey

n meat from a big bird

vegetarian

n

ex Does he eat no meat? Maybe he is a vegetarian.

We are close

We love one another

dining room

n a place for eating in a home

parade

n a line of special cars and people in the street

10 minutes

Part A. Sentence Completion

1. I will drive _______ to Philadelphia tonight.

(A) top
(B) back
(C) front
(D) behind

2. _______ I play, Mom waters the plants.

(A) But
(B) And
(C) Why
(D) While

Part B. Situational Writing

3.

Betsy is _______.

(A) cooking food
(B) washing dishes
(C) cleaning her car
(D) shopping at the store

4.

Takeshi is a vegetarian. So he doesn't eat _______.

(A) tofu
(B) food
(C) meat
(D) vegetables

Part C. Practical Reading and Retelling

Thanksgiving Dinner Menu

We are open on Thanksgiving Day! If your family is too far away, come and eat here. We serve Thanksgiving dinner!

Roasted turkey for one person - $15
Fried turkey for one person - $17
Vegetarian pasta for one person - $13

*Every turkey dish includes 2 side dishes

Side dishes

Mashed potatoes	Fried mushrooms
Baked sweet potatoes	Bread
Tofu salad	Pasta and cheese
Green beans	

5. How much is a vegetarian meal for one person?

(A) $13
(B) $15
(C) $17
(D) $19

6. What is NOT a side dish?

(A) tofu salad
(B) fried turkey
(C) green beans
(D) mashed potatoes

Part D. General Reading and Retelling

My mom, dad, and I live in New York. But my grandparents, aunts, uncles, and cousins live in Detroit. Every Thanksgiving, we travel to Detroit. My dad drives us to Detroit. It takes about 10 hours. When we get to Grandma and Grandpa's house, the adults start cooking food. My mom cooks turkey and sweet potatoes. My aunts make cornbread and apple pies. Grandma washes the dishes. My dad makes tofu salad and fruit dishes. Those dishes are for the vegetarians in the family. Vegetarians don't eat meat. Grandma is a vegetarian.

While the adults cook, the kids stay in the living room. We are all very close to one another. We play board games and card games. I like card games more because I always win. This year, my cousin Amy brought video games. So we took turns playing them. My cousin James won every game! After three hours, Grandma said, "____________________" So we all went to the dining room and sat down to eat. There was a lot of food, but we ate it all! After dinner, we watched TV in the living room. We watched a parade on TV. It was very fun. Then we went to sleep. We have to drive back to New York tomorrow!

7. What does the writer say about Grandma?

(A) She is very sick.
(B) She does not eat meat.
(C) She plays video games.
(D) She cooks delicious food.

8. What is NOT a dish the family cooked?

(A) turkey
(B) chicken
(C) apple pie
(D) tofu salad

9. Who was the best at playing video games?

(A) Amy
(B) James
(C) the writer
(D) Grandpa

10. Which sentence goes best in the blank?

(A) Dinner is ready!
(B) Come help us cook!
(C) Go play video games!
(D) This is really delicious!

Listening Practice

Listen and write.

MP3 B3-5

Thanksgiving in Detroit

My mom, dad, and I live in New York. But my grandparents, aunts, uncles, and cousins live in Detroit. Every Thanksgiving, we travel to Detroit. My dad drives us to Detroit. It takes about 10 hours. When we get to Grandma and Grandpa's house, the [1] ____________ start cooking food. My mom cooks [2] ____________ and sweet potatoes. My aunts make cornbread and apple pies. Grandma washes the dishes. My dad makes tofu salad and fruit dishes. Those dishes are for the vegetarians in the family. Vegetarians don't eat meat. Grandma is a [3] ____________. While the adults cook, the kids stay in the living room. We are all very [4] ____________ to one another. We play board games and card games. I like card games more because I always win. This year, my cousin Amy bought video games. So we took turns playing them. My cousin James won every game! After three hours, Grandma said, "Dinner is ready!" So we all went to the [5] ____________ room and sat down to eat. There was a lot of food, but we ate it all! After dinner, we watched TV in the living room. We watched a [6] ____________ on TV. It was very fun. Then we went to sleep. We have to drive back to New York tomorrow!

Word Bank

adults	dinning	closse
close	vegetarian	tukey
parade	vegtarian	dining
turkey	perade	adolts

Listen. Pause. Say each sentence.

MP3 B3-5G

Writing Practice

Write the words.

1 ____________

n not a baby or child

2 ____________

n meat from a big bird

3 ____________

n

ex Does he eat no meat? Maybe he is a ______.

4 ____________

We love one another

5 ____________

n a place for eating in a home

6 ____________

n a line of special cars and people in the street

Write the words in each blank.

Summary

Every Thanksgiving, my family goes to see my ____________. The drive is ____________ hours. We cook and ____________ a lot. Some of us eat meat, and some are ____________. We play cards and watch TV.

Word Puzzle

Complete the word puzzle.

1 ↓
We love one another

3 ↓
a place for eating
in a home

2 →
not a baby or child

4 ↓
Does he eat no meat?
Maybe he is a ______.

5 →
a line of special cars
and people in the street

6 →
meat from a big bird

Teacher's Book p.180

UNIT 6

Siesta

Think about your town. When do shops open and close?

UNIT 6 Siesta

Jessica has to work now, but she went to bed late last night. She is tired, and she wants to take a nap. She remembers a story. Her friend Juana told her the story. Juana lives in Spain now. Juana talked about the "siesta." The siesta is famous in Spanish culture, but what is it? It is a work break during the day. During the siesta, shops close, so people can take a nap. The siesta time for shops is from 2 PM to 5 PM. People go to restaurants to eat. Then they rest. So the siesta time for restaurants is from 4 PM to 8 PM. Jessica asked, "Why do people enjoy the siesta in Spain?" Juana continued with her story. Spain is a hot country. Many workers enjoy a break when it is very hot, around 2 PM. After 5 PM, the weather becomes cooler, and people can work again. Jessica asked again, "Shops now can cool their air. Why do people need a siesta?" Juana said, "Maybe they don't. These days, many people do not take a siesta."

New Words

go to bed late v lie down in bed to sleep at a late hour	break n a rest
take a nap v go to sleep a short time during the day	continue with your story v keep telling your story
cool v make colder	these days adv nowadays

10 minutes

Part A. Sentence Completion

1. _______ is very hot today.

(A) I

(B) It

(C) Those

(D) Today

2. Sam went to the market _______ some fruit.

(A) buys

(B) buyer

(C) to buy

(D) bought

Part B. Situational Writing

3.

It is time to _______ bed.

(A) go to

(B) ship the

(C) make the

(D) come from

4.

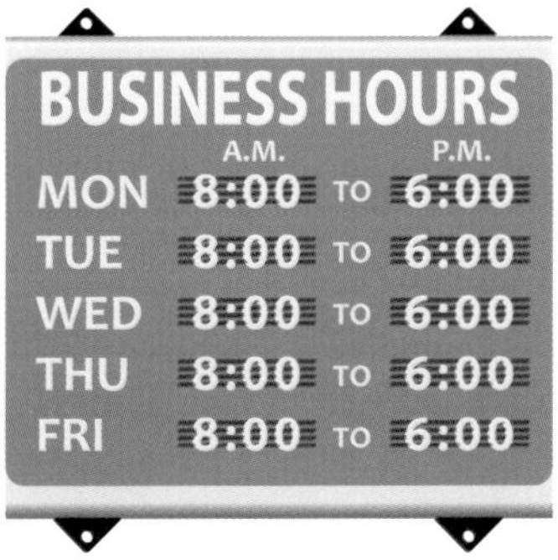

It is Monday at 7:00 PM. The shop is _______.

(A) full

(B) open

(C) closed

(D) popular

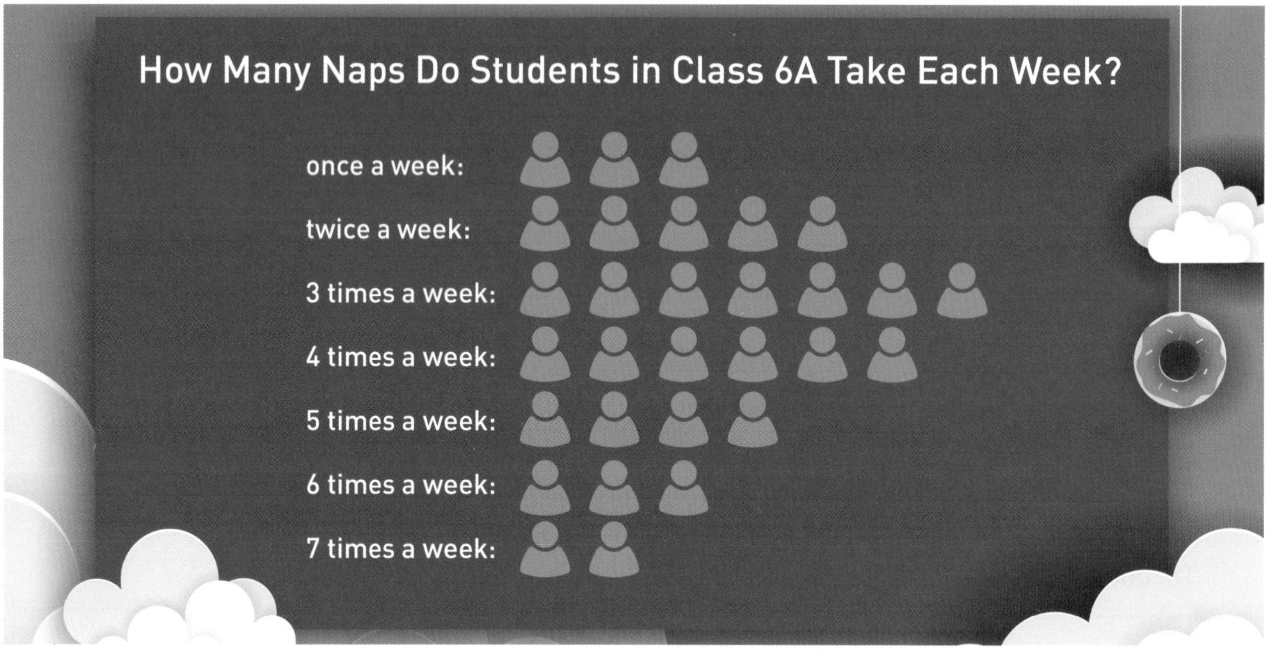

5. How many students take naps four times a week?

(A) 3
(B) 4
(C) 5
(D) 6

6. Which of the following is NOT true?

(A) The class has 25 students.
(B) Two students take a nap every day.
(C) Some students take a nap on weekends.
(D) All students take a nap at least one time a week.

Part D. General Reading and Retelling

Jessica has to work now, but she went to bed late last night. She is tired, and she wants to take a nap. She remembers a story. Her friend Juana told her the story. Juana lives in Spain now. Juana talked about the "siesta." The siesta is famous in Spanish culture, but what is it? It is a work break during the day. During the siesta, shops close, so people can take a nap. The siesta time for shops is from 2 PM to 5 PM. People go to restaurants to eat. Then they rest. So the siesta time for restaurants is from 4 PM to 8 PM. Jessica asked, "Why do people enjoy the siesta in Spain?" Juana continued with her story. Spain is a hot country. Many workers enjoy a break when it is very hot, around 2 PM. After 5 PM, the weather becomes cooler, and people can work again. Jessica asked again, "Shops now can cool their air. Why do people need a siesta?" Juana said, "Maybe they don't. These days, many people do not take a siesta."

7. What is the main idea of the passage?
   - (A) The food in Spain is delicious.
   - (B) Jessica and Juana are best friends.
   - (C) Jessica and Juana always rest after lunch.
   - (D) Spanish people have a siesta for a reason.

8. What is NOT true about Juana?
   - (A) She lives in Spain.
   - (B) She is Jessica's friend.
   - (C) She knows what a siesta is.
   - (D) She thinks everyone needs a siesta.

9. According to Juana, when is the siesta for restaurants?
   - (A) 2 PM to 5 PM
   - (B) 4 PM to 8 PM
   - (C) After 5 PM
   - (D) After 8 PM

10. According to Juana, why do people take siestas?
    - (A) Some people are lazy.
    - (B) The weather is very hot.
    - (C) People don't need breaks.
    - (D) Spanish meals are heavy.

Listening Practice

Listen and write.

MP3 B3-6

Siesta

Jessica has to work now, but she [1] ______________ late last night. She is tired, and she wants to [2] ______________. She remembers a story. Her friend Juana told her the story. Juana lives in Spain now. Juana talked about the "siesta." The siesta is famous in Spanish culture, but what is it? It is a work [3] ______________ during the day. During the siesta, shops close, so people can take a nap. The siesta time for shops is from 2 PM to 5 PM. People go to restaurants to eat. Then they rest. So the siesta time for restaurants is from 4 PM to 8 PM. Jessica asked, "Why do people enjoy the siesta in Spain?" Juana [4] ______________ with her story. Spain is a hot country. Many workers enjoy a break when it is very hot, around 2 PM. After 5 PM, the weather becomes cooler, and people can work again. Jessica asked again, "Shops now can [5] ______________ their air. Why do people need a siesta?" Juana said, "Maybe they don't. [6] ______________, many people do not take a siesta."

Word Bank

brake	kool	These days
continued	contnued	went a bed
take a nap	break	went to bed
cool	Thesedays	take nap

Listen. Pause. Say each sentence.

MP3 B3-6G

Writing Practice

Write the words.

1 ________________ *v* lie down in bed to sleep at a late hour	2 ________________ *n* a rest
3 ________________ *v* go to sleep a short time during the day	4 ________________ *v* keep telling your story
5 ________________ *v* make colder	6 ________________ *adv* nowadays

Write the words in each blank.

Summary

In Spain, the “siesta” is a ________________ in the day. It started due to ________________ weather. Shops and ________________ close. But ________________, not everyone does the siesta.

Word Puzzle

Complete the word puzzle.

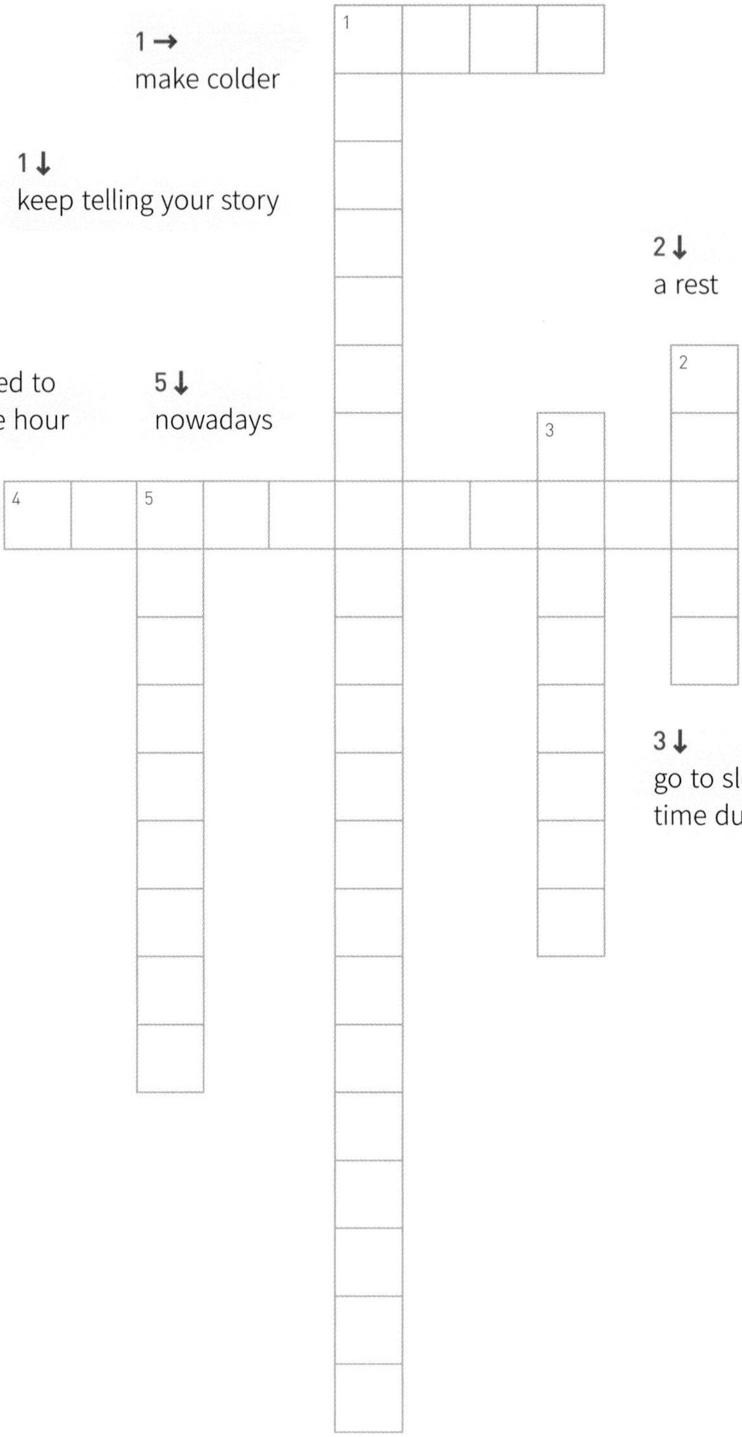

1 → make colder

1 ↓ keep telling your story

2 ↓ a rest

3 ↓ go to sleep a short time during the day

4 → lie down in bed to sleep at a late hour

5 ↓ nowadays

Teacher's Book p.185

UNIT 7

The Mystery of King Tut

What does "pharaoh" mean?
Can you name a pharaoh of ancient Egypt?

UNIT 7 The Mystery of King Tut

King Tut was a famous king in Egypt. He was called a "pharaoh." Pharaoh means king. Pharaohs ruled Egypt. Why was King Tut so famous? Because his body was in a very clean and tidy tomb. A tomb is a place for a dead body. Modern people could study the tomb. They could learn about King Tut's life.

Howard Carter found King Tut's tomb in 1922. Carter studied old history. How old was King Tut's body? About 3,200 years old! There were many treasures in the area. It became famous very quickly. Then people had a question. How did King Tut die? He died young. He was only 19 when he died. Some people think he was ill. Others say an animal bit him. Professor Albert Zink is from Italy. He believes King Tut was always weak – even as a baby. Zink did some tests on King Tut's family. The tests looked at King Tut's parents. The parents were brother and sister. Maybe that made a weak baby, but nobody really knows how King Tut died. We only know he was young.

New Words

tidy *adj* clean and neat	tomb *n* a grave
modern *adj* not old	treasure *n* a special, valuable thing
ill *adj* sick	weak *adj* not strong

Part A. Sentence Completion

1. _______ is your sister?

(A) How old
(B) How long
(C) How often
(D) How many

2. Albert Einstein was _______ Germany.

(A) to
(B) on
(C) from
(D) about

Part B. Situational Writing

3.

The dog _______.

(A) bit the robber
(B) kicked the man
(C) hugged the owner
(D) danced on the floor

4.

The room was messy but now it is _______.

(A) pink
(B) tidy
(C) weak
(D) young

5. John is 7 years old. How much is the ticket for John?

(A) $5

(B) $10

(C) $20

(D) John cannot have a ticket.

6. What should you do in the tomb?

(A) be quiet

(B) take pictures

(C) bring babies

(D) touch the pharaoh

Part D. General Reading and Retelling

King Tut was a famous king in Egypt. He was called a "pharaoh." Pharaoh means king. Pharaohs ruled Egypt. Why was King Tut so famous? Because his body was in a very clean and tidy tomb. A tomb is a place for a dead body. Modern people could study the tomb. They could learn about King Tut's life.

Howard Carter found King Tut's tomb in 1922. Carter studied old history. How old was King Tut's body? About 3,200 years old! There were many treasures in the area. It became famous very quickly. Then people had a question. How did King Tut die? He died young. He was only 19 when he died. Some people think he was ill. Others say an animal bit him. Professor Albert Zink is from Italy. He believes King Tut was always weak — even as a baby. Zink did some tests on King Tut's family. The tests looked at King Tut's parents. The parents were brother and sister. Maybe that made a weak baby, but nobody really knows how King Tut died. We only know he was young.

7. What is the best title for the passage?
   (A) Facts about King Tut
   (B) All the Kings of Egypt
   (C) How to Test Old People
   (D) Pharaohs Work Very Hard

8. According to the passage, what did pharaohs do?
   (A) rule Egypt
   (B) steal treasure
   (C) hide old tombs
   (D) study old history

9. Which is mentioned about King Tut's death?
   (A) A rock hit him.
   (B) An animal bit him.
   (C) He fell from a tree.
   (D) He fell into a fast river.

10. What did Albert Zink do?
   (A) find King Tut's tomb
   (B) die when he was 19
   (C) test King Tut's family
   (D) make King Tut famous

Listening Practice

Listen and write.

MP3 B3-7

The Mystery of King Tut

King Tut was a famous king in Egypt. He was called a "pharaoh." Pharaoh means king. Pharaohs ruled Egypt. Why was King Tut so famous? Because his body was in a very clean and [1] ______ tomb. A tomb is a place for a dead body. [2] ______ people could study the [3] ______. They could learn about King Tut's life.

Howard Carter found King Tut's tomb in 1922. Carter studied old history. How old was King Tut's body? About 3,200 years old! There were many [4] ______ in the area. It became famous very quickly. Then people had a question. How did King Tut die? He died young. He was only 19 when he died. Some people think he was [5] ______. Others say an animal bit him. Professor Albert Zink is from Italy. He believes King Tut was always [6] ______ – even as a baby. Zink did some tests on King Tut's family. The tests looked at King Tut's parents. The parents were brother and sister. Maybe that made a weak baby, but nobody really knows how King Tut died. We only know he was young.

Word Bank

weak	ill	Morden
tresures	treasures	Modern
ell	tumb	week
tidy	tidi	tomb

Listen. Pause. Say each sentence.

MP3 B3-7G

Writing Practice

Write the words.

1 ______________ *adj* clean and neat	2 ______________ *n* a grave
3 ______________ *adj* not old	4 ______________ *n* a special, valuable thing
5 ______________ *adj* sick	6 ______________ *adj* not strong

Write the words in each blank.

Summary

King Tut was a famous king in ______________. Modern people could ______________ about his life by studying his old ______________. But no one knows why he ______________ so young.

Word Puzzle

Complete the word puzzle.

1↓
a special, valuable thing

1→
a grave

2→
not strong

3→
not old

4→
clean and neat

5↓
sick

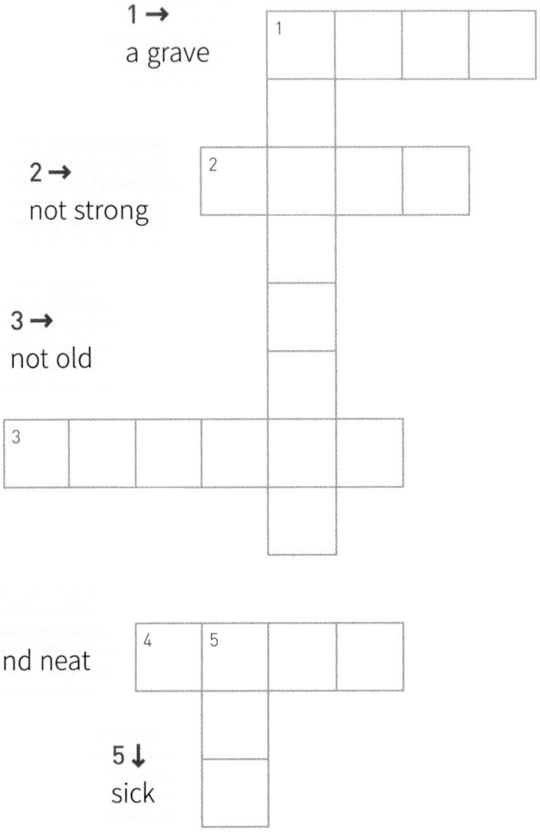

Teacher's Book p.189

UNIT 8

The History of the Mexican Flag

What country is this flag from?
Can you draw your country's national flag?

UNIT 8 The History of the Mexican Flag

February 24th is a special day for Mexicans. On February 24th, 1984, Mexico chose its modern flag. The Mexican flag has three wide stripes. The stripes are green, white, and red. The green stripe is on the left. The white one is in the middle. And the red one is on the right. Each color has a meaning. Green is for hope. White is about being together. Red is like the blood of heroes. There are also pictures on the middle stripe. The white stripe has an eagle, a snake, and a cactus. These things show Mexico's special story. In the story, the Aztec people were looking for a place. The place had an eagle, snake, and cactus. Tenoch was an Aztec leader. He found the place and built a city there. The Aztecs called the city Tenochtitlan. Tenochtitlan is now Mexico City, Mexico's capital.

Mexicans had actually used the flag before 1984. Miguel Hidalgo used a similar flag. Hidalgo was a famous Mexican soldier. He fought against Spain. Then President Guadalupe Victoria also used the flag. He took it with him in a war with Spain. The Mexican flag has a long history. However, in 1984, the flag became the national symbol by law. This is why February 24th is Flag Day in Mexico.

New Words

wide *adj* not narrow	**stripe** *n* a thick line
cactus *n* a desert plant 	**capital** *n* the main city in a country
similar *adj* almost the same	**soldier** *n* a warrior

Part A. Sentence Completion

1. ________ is New Year's Day your favorite holiday? Is it because of the fireworks?

(A) Why
(B) Who
(C) When
(D) Where

2. France fought ________ England in 1754.

(A) to
(B) war
(C) against
(D) together

Part B. Situational Writing

3.

The phone on the right is ________.

(A) older
(B) smaller
(C) more black
(D) more modern

4.

They are ________.

(A) soldiers
(B) teachers
(C) firefighters
(D) pharmacists

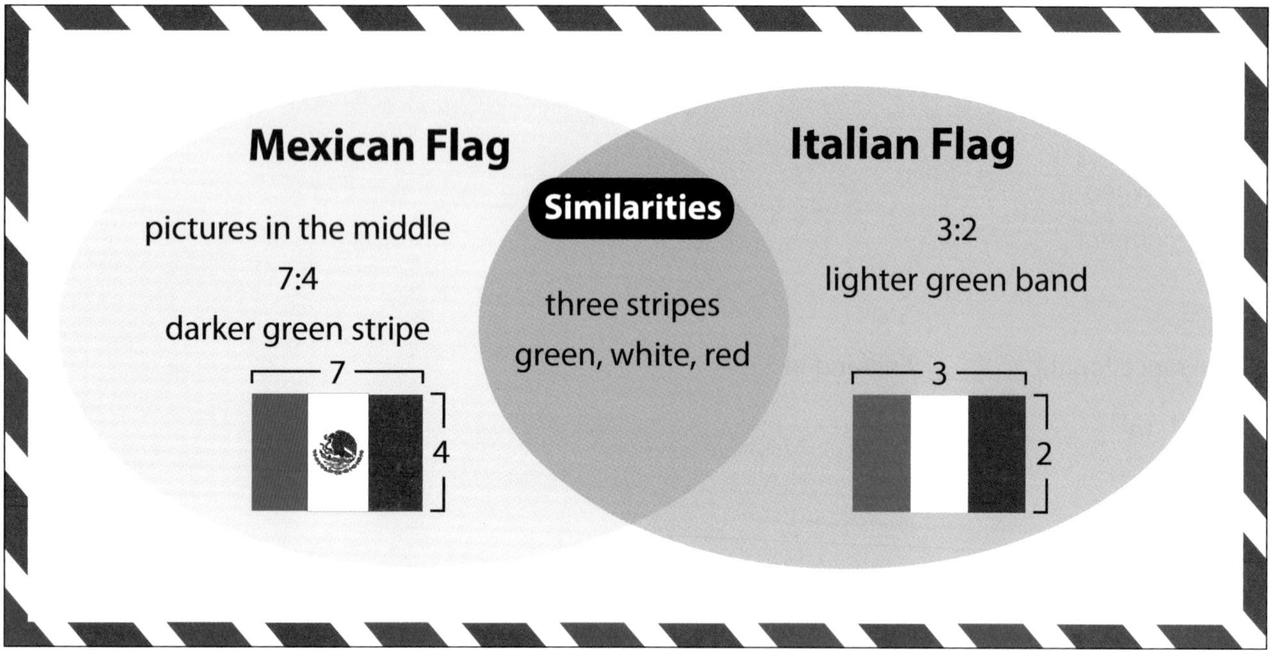

5. According to the diagram, what is NOT the same for the Mexican and Italian flags?

(A) three stripes

(B) a green band

(C) pictures in the middle

(D) a red band on the right

6. What does the diagram say about the Italian flag?

(A) It has a ratio of 7:4.

(B) It has a lighter green band.

(C) It has a darker green band.

(D) It has pictures in the middle.

Part D. General Reading and Retelling

February 24th is a special day for Mexicans. On February 24th, 1984, Mexico chose its modern flag. The Mexican flag has three wide stripes. The stripes are green, white, and red. The green stripe is on the left. The white one is in the middle. And the red one is on the right. Each color has a meaning. Green is for hope. White is about being together. Red is like the blood of heroes. There are also pictures on the middle stripe. The white stripe has an eagle, a snake, and a cactus. These things show Mexico's special story. In the story, the Aztec people were looking for a place. The place had an eagle, snake, and cactus. Tenoch was an Aztec leader. He found the place and built a city there. The Aztecs called the city Tenochtitlan. Tenochtitlan is now Mexico City, Mexico's capital.

Mexicans had actually used the flag before 1984. Miguel Hidalgo used a similar flag. Hidalgo was a famous Mexican soldier. He fought against Spain. Then President Guadalupe Victoria also used the flag. He took it with him in a war with Spain. The Mexican flag has a long history. However, in 1984, the flag became the national symbol by law. This is why February 24th is Flag Day in Mexico.

7. What is the best title for the passage?
   - (A) Animals in Mexico City
   - (B) Ways to Celebrate Flag Day
   - (C) The History of the Mexican Flag
   - (D) How Guadalupe Became the President

8. According to the passage, what is NOT true about the Mexican flag?
   - (A) It has three stripes.
   - (B) Red is for the heroes.
   - (C) Green means being together.
   - (D) It became the national flag in 1984.

9. What is NOT on the flag?
   - (A) a snake
   - (B) a cactus
   - (C) an eagle
   - (D) a person

10. Who was Miguel Hidalgo?
    - (A) an Aztec leader
    - (B) a Mexican soldier
    - (C) a Spanish general
    - (D) the first president of Mexico

Listening Practice

Listen and write.

MP3 B3-8

The History of the Mexican Flag

February 24th is a special day for Mexicans. On February 24th, 1984, Mexico chose its modern flag. The Mexican flag has three [1] ________ stripes. The stripes are green, white, and red. The green [2] ________ is on the left. The white one is in the middle. And the red one is on the right. Each color has a meaning. Green is for hope. White is about being together. Red is like the blood of heroes. There are also pictures on the middle stripe. The white stripe has an eagle, a snake, and a [3] ________. These things show Mexico's special story. In the story, the Aztec people were looking for a place. The place had an eagle, snake, and cactus. Tenoch was an Aztec leader. He found the place and built a city there. The Aztecs called the city Tenochtitlan. Tenochtitlan is now Mexico City, Mexico's [4] ________. Mexicans had actually used the flag before 1984. Miguel Hidalgo used a [5] ________ flag. Hidalgo was a famous Mexican [6] ________. He fought against Spain. Then President Guadalupe Victoria also used the flag. He took it with him in a war with Spain. The Mexican flag has a long history. However, in 1984, the flag became the national symbol by law. This is why February 24th is Flag Day in Mexico.

Word Bank

cactus	kaktus	wid
similar	soldier	simmilar
strip	stripe	capitel
wide	capital	soljur

Listen. Pause. Say each sentence.

MP3 B3-8G

Writing Practice

Write the words.

1 ____________ *adj* not narrow	2 ____________ *n* a thick line
3 ____________ *n* a desert plant 	4 ____________ *n* the main city in a country
5 ____________ *adj* almost the same	6 ____________ *n* a warrior

Write the words in each blank.

Summary

Mexico chose its modern ____________ on February 24th, 1984. The ____________ flag has wide green, ____________, and red stripes. It also has an eagle, a ____________, and a cactus.

Word Puzzle

Complete the word puzzle.

1↓
a thick line

3↓
a desert plant

2↓
almost the same

4→
not narrow

5→
the main city in a country

6→
a warrior

CHAPTER REVIEW

Learning the Culture of Planet 182

Teacher's Book p.194

An alien named Blorg lived on Planet 97. One day, she decided to go on a trip to Planet 182. When she arrived there, she was very surprised. The hotel workers said "hello" to Blorg by waving their feet! Then, Blorg went into a restaurant. Inside, aliens were eating food with their toes. Some were also reading books and using computers with their feet. She asked a local alien, "Why do you use your feet for everything?" He answered, "Feet are an important part of the body. Using the feet helps your brain and makes you smarter." At first, Blorg could not understand. But then, she stayed on Planet 182 for a month. She used her feet to eat, write, and brush her teeth. After a month, she thought, "I feel much smarter!" She began to love using her feet. After a month, Blorg returned to Planet 97. There, she kept using her feet to do some things every day.

CHAPTER 3

Nature & the Earth

Teacher's Book
p.195

UNIT 9

Eric's Book about Habitats

Name three animals. Where do they live?

UNIT 9 Eric's Book about Habitats

Last week was reading week at Hyden Elementary School. During reading week, all students visit the library every day. Students choose and read books there. Eric read a book called "Animals and their Habitats." He is interested in learning about animals.

At first, Eric didn't know the meaning of the word "habitat." So he asked his mom, Helen. Helen is a scientist and studies animal habitats. That's why she knows a lot about different animals and where they live. Helen is always reading books about animals. Helen told Eric that a habitat is a place for animals and plants. Animals and plants live in a habitat. So it is like a home!

How do animals choose habitats? They choose by need. The needs are air, water, food, and space. For example, fish live in the sea. That's because they need water. Sharks and sea turtles live in the ocean, too. They live in the same habitat as fish.

Eric liked learning about habitats. He wants to learn more. Do dogs and cats have a habitat? What about birds? Tomorrow, Eric will get more books and learn more.

New Words

habitat
n a home area for animals and plants

be interested in V-ing
v want to V

scientist
n a science worker

need
n a necessary thing

space
n room

shark
n a large fish with big teeth

10 minutes

Part A. Sentence Completion

1. Liuwei _______ in reading books.

(A) interests
(B) interesting
(C) is interested
(D) is interesting

2. _______ are swimming in the sea.

(A) Fish
(B) Seal
(C) A fish
(D) A seal

Part B. Situational Writing

3. 

Ben tries to _______.

(A) do chores
(B) study hard
(C) water trees
(D) help an animal

4. 

My grandmother is a _______.

(A) cook
(B) florist
(C) pianist
(D) scientist

5. Delar will draw a rainforest poster. What kind of animal should he draw?

(A) a frog

(B) a seal

(C) a camel

(D) a polar bear

6. According to the poster, which animals share the same habitat?

(A) sharks and bears

(B) camels and seals

(C) deer and squirrels

(D) frogs and beluga whales

Part D. General Reading and Retelling

Last week was reading week at Hyden Elementary School. During reading week, all students visit the library every day. Students choose and read books there. Eric read a book called "Animals and their Habitats." He is interested in learning about animals.
At first, Eric didn't know the meaning of the word "habitat." So he asked his mom, Helen. Helen is a scientist and studies animal habitats. That's why she knows a lot about different animals and where they live. Helen is always reading books about animals. Helen told Eric that a habitat is a place for animals and plants. Animals and plants live in a habitat. So it is like a home!
How do animals choose habitats? They choose by need. The needs are air, water, food, and space. For example, fish live in the sea. That's because they need water. Sharks and sea turtles live in the ocean, too. They live in the same habitat as fish.
Eric liked learning about habitats. He wants to learn more. Do dogs and cats have a habitat? What about birds? Tomorrow, Eric will get more books and learn more.

7. What is the best title for the passage?

(A) Eric's Pet Fish
(B) Eric Teaches Helen
(C) Eric Dislikes Reading
(D) Eric Learns about Habitat

8. Where do the students read books during reading week?

(A) at home
(B) in the gym
(C) in the library
(D) in the classroom

9. What is a habitat?

(A) a reading week
(B) a place for books
(C) a food for animals
(D) a home for animals

10. According to the story, which animals share a habitat?

(A) Eric, sharks, cats
(B) dogs, fish, sea turtles
(C) Helen, fish, sea turtles
(D) sharks, fish, sea turtles

Listening Practice

Listen and write.

MP3 B3-9

Eric's Book about Habitats

Last week was reading week at Hyden Elementary School. During reading week, all students visit the library every day. Students choose and read books there. Eric read a book called "Animals and their Habitats." He is [1] ________ learning about animals.

At first, Eric didn't know the meaning of the word "[2] ________." So he asked his mom, Helen. Helen is a [3] ________ and studies animal habitats. That's why she knows a lot about different animals and where they live. Helen is always reading books about animals. Helen told Eric that a habitat is a place for animals and plants. Animals and plants live in a habitat. So it is like a home!

How do animals choose habitats? They choose by [4] ________. The needs are air, water, food, and [5] ________. For example, fish live in the sea. That's because they need water. [6] ________ and sea turtles live in the ocean, too. They live in the same habitat as fish.

Eric liked learning about habitats. He wants to learn more. Do dogs and cats have a habitat? What about birds? Tomorrow, Eric will get more books and learn more.

Word Bank

need	interested in	interestedin
Shaks	habitat	needed
sientist	Sharks	hebitat
space	spase	scientist

Listen. Pause. Say each sentence.

MP3 B3-9G

Writing Practice

Write the words.

1 ______________ *n* a home area for animals and plants	2 ______________ V-ing *v* want to V
3 ______________ *n* a science worker	4 ______________ *n* a necessary thing
5 ______________ *n* room	6 ______________ *n* a large fish with big teeth 

Write the words in each blank.

Summary

Eric learned about habitats. A ______________ is where animals and ______________ live. Animals choose their habitat by the things they need, such as ______________, water, ______________ and space.

Word Puzzle

Complete the word puzzle.

1↓
want to V

2↓
a home area for animals and plants

3→
a science worker

4↓
room

4→
a large fish with big teeth

5→
a necessary thing

Teacher's Book p.199

UNIT 10

Global Warming: The Sahara

What is global warming?
Name a problem from global warming.

UNIT 10 Global Warming: The Sahara

The earth is becoming hot very fast. This is called global warming. Ice is melting, the ocean is getting bigger, and animals are dying. Who is making the earth hot and sick? Scientists say it is us. Humans cause global warming. Here is one big problem with global warming in Africa. The Sahara Desert in Africa is the world's biggest hot desert. Some scientists found that it is getting bigger every year. This means there is less water in Africa. Why is the Sahara Desert becoming bigger? There are two big reasons. First, the weather is changing, and it doesn't rain as much anymore. The weather is changing because of global warming. So humans are causing weather changes. Second, people are using lakes by the desert for their plants. They use too much water from the lakes. So the lakes are getting smaller. Lake Chad is one of these lakes. Sadly, other deserts are getting bigger, too. In the future, people will not have enough water. To stop this problem, the weather should stop changing. To stop the changing weather, global warming must stop.

New Words

global warming *n* planet Earth getting warmer	**melt** *v* Is your ice cream in the sun? Maybe it is melting. 
human *n* a person	**desert** *n* a hot, dry, sandy place
get bigger *v* become bigger	**lake** *n* a place with fresh water

10 minutes

Part A. Sentence Completion

1. She is exercising, so she is _______ stronger every day.

(A) get
(B) got
(C) gets
(D) getting

2. I'm hungry because I didn't have _______ for lunch.

(A) too food
(B) food must
(C) enough food
(D) food enough

Part B. Situational Writing

3.

The green fish is _______ than the yellow fish.

(A) bigger
(B) smaller
(C) shorter
(D) cheaper

4.

The snowman is _______.

(A) drying
(B) melting
(C) waving
(D) jogging

Part C. Practical Reading and Retelling

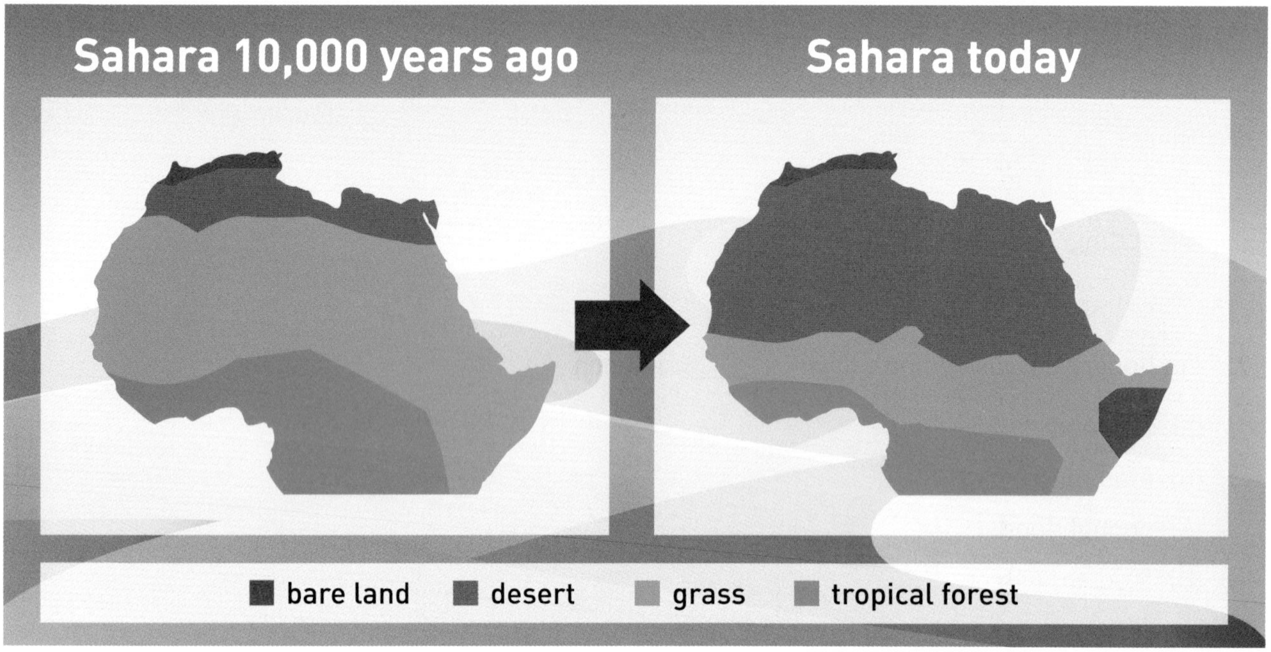

5. According to the picture, what happened to the tropical forest?

   (A) It became bigger.
   (B) It became smaller.
   (C) It stayed the same.
   (D) It became bigger than the desert.

6. According to the picture, which land grew the most?

   (A) grass
   (B) desert
   (C) bare land
   (D) tropical forest

Part D. General Reading and Retelling

The earth is becoming hot very fast. This is called global warming. Ice is melting, the ocean is getting bigger, and animals are dying. Who is making the earth hot and sick? Scientists say it is us. Humans cause global warming. Here is one big problem with global warming in Africa. The Sahara Desert in Africa is the world's biggest hot desert. Some scientists found that it is getting bigger every year. This means there is less water in Africa. Why is the Sahara Desert becoming bigger? There are two big reasons. First, the weather is changing, and it doesn't rain as much anymore. The weather is changing because of global warming. So humans are causing weather changes. Second, people are using lakes by the desert for their plants. They use too much water from the ________. So the lakes are getting smaller. Lake Chad is one of these lakes. Sadly, other deserts are getting bigger, too. In the future, people will not have enough water. To stop this problem, the weather should stop changing. To stop the changing weather, global warming must stop.

7. What is the best title for the passage?

   (A) A Trip to the Sahara Desert
   (B) Scientists Study Nature in Africa
   (C) People Love Swimming in Lake Chad
   (D) Global Warming is a Big Problem in Africa

8. According to the passage, what is the problem of the Sahara Desert?

   (A) It has no animals.
   (B) It rains too much.
   (C) It is getting bigger.
   (D) It has too many visitors.

9. What is NOT true about the Sahara Desert?

   (A) It is in Africa.
   (B) It has lakes close to it.
   (C) It causes global warming.
   (D) It is the biggest hot desert.

10. Which word goes best in the blank?

   (A) rivers
   (B) lakes
   (C) plants
   (D) people

Listening Practice

Listen and write.

MP3 B3-10

Global Warming: The Sahara

The earth is becoming hot very fast. This is called [1] ________ warming. Ice is [2] ________, the ocean is getting bigger, and animals are dying. Who is making the earth hot and sick? Scientists say it is us. Humans cause global warming. Here is one big problem with global warming in Africa. The Sahara Desert in Africa is the world's biggest hot [3] ________. Some scientists found that it is getting [4] ________ every year. This means there is less water in Africa. Why is the Sahara Desert becoming bigger? There are two big reasons. First, the weather is changing, and it doesn't rain as much anymore. The weather is changing because of global warming. So [5] ________ are causing weather changes. Second, people are using lakes by the desert for their plants. They use too much water from the lakes. So the lakes are getting smaller. Lake Chad is one of these [6] ________. Sadly, other deserts are getting bigger, too. In the future, people will not have enough water. To stop this problem, the weather should stop changing. To stop the changing weather, global warming must stop.

Word Bank

meltting	bigger	lakes
globar	humans	biger
homans	melting	global
dessert	desert	laks

Listen. Pause. Say each sentence.

MP3 B3-10G

Writing Practice

Write the words.

1 ____________

n planet Earth getting warmer

2 ____________

v Is your ice cream in the sun? Maybe it is ______ing.

3 ____________

n a person

4 ____________

n a hot, dry, sandy place

5 ____________

v become bigger

6 ____________

n a place with fresh water

Write the words in each blank.

Summary

The Sahara Desert is getting even ____________ every year. There are ____________ main reasons. First, global ____________ means less rain. Second, people are using too much ____________ from nearby lakes.

Word Puzzle

Complete the word puzzle.

1↓
Is your ice cream in the sun? Maybe it is _______ing.

2↓
a hot, dry, sandy place

3→
become bigger

3↓
planet Earth getting warmer

4→
a place with fresh water

5→
a person

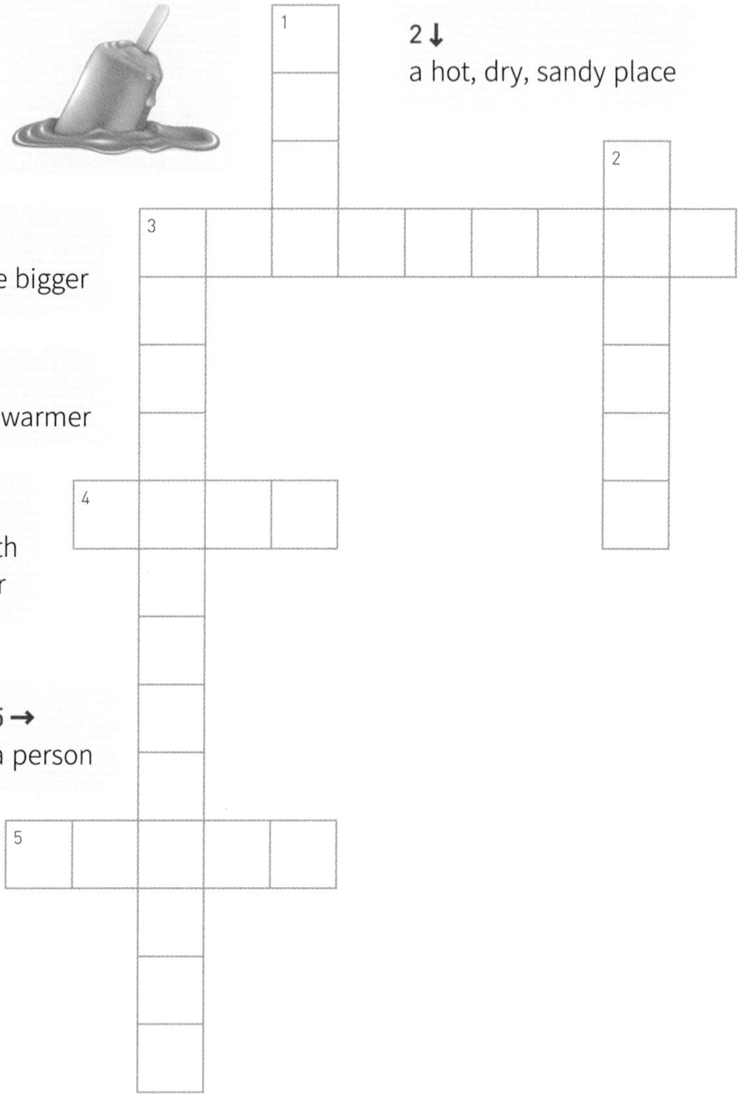

Teacher's Book p.204

UNIT 11

Three Ways to Save the Earth

Describe things you do to save the earth.

UNIT 11 Three Ways to Save the Earth

How do you feel when you hear the word "earth"? The earth is like our parent, because it gives everything to us. It gives us food, a home, and clothes. So we must save our parent by following these tips. We can save the trees, water, land, and even ourselves. First, we must save water. We cannot live without water. At home, we can turn off the water when we are not using it. We should turn it off when we brush our teeth. And we should wash our clothes in cold water. Second, we must save trees. Trees give us clean air. Let's not use paper cups. We should use glasses and wash them. Then, we can use them again! We should also not use too much paper. We should print on both sides of a piece of paper. Finally, we should save energy. We must turn off the lights when we leave a room. We should turn off our computers when we are not using them. Doing those things can help save money, too. Everyone should try to save the earth. Why? Because it is everyone's parent. Let's keep the earth safe.

New Words

brush your teeth

v use a toothbrush and toothpaste to clean your teeth

turn off (the water; the lights)

v stop

print

v

ex Do you need a paper copy? Then you should <u>print</u> it.

glass

n a tall cup made of glass

leave X

v go out of X

parent

n mother or father

10 minutes

Part A. Sentence Completion

1. I cannot eat soup _______ a spoon.

(A) out

(B) with it

(C) without

(D) with you

2. Does this plant need _______ sunlight?

(A) few

(B) two

(C) four

(D) much

Part B. Situational Writing

3.

The girl is _______.

(A) swimming in a lake

(B) recycling a paper cup

(C) drinking a glass of water

(D) putting down a glass cup

4.

Every night, Khalid _______ the light.

(A) puts in

(B) lifts up

(C) turns off

(D) puts down

Part C. **Practical Reading and Retelling**

Dear Earth,

I'm very sorry. You are like my mother or father.
You gave life to me, but I was not nice to you.
I threw garbage on the ground.
I picked flowers because they are beautiful.
I used plastic cups, dishes, and forks.
Now I will be nice to you. I will take care of you.
Thank you for giving me everything!

Fadi Bloch

5. According to the letter, what did Fadi NOT do?

   (A) pick flowers
   (B) use plastic dishes
   (C) take care of the Earth
   (D) throw garbage on the ground

6. According to the letter, what did Earth do for Fadi?

   (A) give life to Fadi
   (B) treat Fadi meanly
   (C) make plastic cups
   (D) take away everything

Part D. General Reading and Retelling

How do you feel when you hear the word "earth"? The earth is like our parent, because it gives everything to us. It gives us food, a home, and clothes. So we must save our parent by following these tips. We can save the trees, water, land, and even ourselves. First, we must save water. We cannot live without water. At home, we can turn off the water when we are not using it. We should turn it off when we brush our teeth. And we should wash our clothes in cold water. Second, we must save trees. Trees give us clean air. Let's not use paper cups. We should use glasses and wash them. Then, we can use them again! We should also not use too much paper. We should print on both sides of a piece of paper. Finally, we should save energy. We must turn off the lights when we leave a room. We should turn off our computers when we are not using them. Doing those things can help save money, too. Everyone should try to save the earth. Why? Because it is everyone's parent. Let's keep the earth safe.

7. What is the main idea of the passage?
   (A) We should help save our planet.
   (B) More trees will bring cleaner air.
   (C) Parents should save their children.
   (D) Drinking too much water is not healthy.

8. According to the passage, what will probably happen when trees are gone?
   (A) The air will become dirty.
   (B) There will be more water.
   (C) There will be no glass cups.
   (D) The earth will be a safe place.

9. Which of the following is NOT mentioned in the passage?
   (A) saving water
   (B) saving trees
   (C) saving energy
   (D) saving clothes

10. According to the passage, why should we use glass cups?
   (A) to use them again
   (B) to throw them away
   (C) to drink more water
   (D) to save kids from getting hurt

Listening Practice

Listen and write.

MP3 B3-11

Three Ways to Save the Earth

How do you feel when you hear the word "earth"? The earth is like our parent, because it gives everything to us. It gives us food, a home, and clothes. So we must save our parent by following these tips. We can save the trees, water, land, and even ourselves. First, we must save water. We cannot live without water. At home, we can [1] ____________ the water when we are not using it. We should turn it off when we [2] ____________ our teeth. And we should wash our clothes in cold water. Second, we must save trees. Trees give us clean air. Let's not use paper cups. We should use [3] ____________ and wash them. Then, we can use them again! We should also not use too much paper. We should [4] ____________ on both sides of a piece of paper. Finally, we should save energy. We must turn off the lights when we [5] ____________ a room. We should turn off our computers when we are not using them. Doing those things can help save money, too. Everyone should try to save the earth. Why? Because it is everyone's [6] ____________. Let's keep the earth safe.

Word Bank

print	grasses	turn off
glasses	turnoff	leave
brus	live	prent
parent	perent	brush

Listen. Pause. Say each sentence.

MP3 B3-11G

Writing Practice

Write the words.

1 ______________ v use a toothbrush and toothpaste to clean your teeth	2 ______________ (the water; the lights) v stop
3 ______________ v ex Do you need a paper copy? Then you should ______ it. 	4 ______________ n a tall cup made of glass 
5 ______________ X v go out of X	6 ______________ n mother or father

Write the words in each blank.

Summary

The ______________ gives us everything. We need to save water, trees, and energy. For example, we should turn off the water when we ______________ our teeth. We also must ______________ the lights when we ______________ the room. Let's keep the earth safe.

Word Puzzle

Complete the word puzzle.

1 ↓
use a toothbrush and toothpaste to clean your teeth

2 →
stop (the water; the lights)

3 →
a tall cup
made of glass

4 →
Do you need a paper copy?
Then you should _______ it.

4 ↓
mother or father

5 →
go out of X

Teacher's Book
p.209

UNIT 12

How Will 2035 Be Different?

Think! What will people eat in the future?

UNIT 12 How Will 2035 Be Different?

What will life be like in 2035? How will it be different? Will there be flying cars, food pills, or a vacation on Mars? Is it going to be like a movie? Sadly, technology may not be that great. It may be less exciting. Technology expert Dean Evans tells you all about it! First, he talks about food. The future of food is greener than today. People will be eating more vegetables and less meat. That's because people will start to eat healthier. People will eat more insects, too. In parts of Asia, people are already eating insects. That's because insects are low in fat. What about the future of health? Will doctors cure everyone who has cancer? No, but there is good news! People will be able to check their health at home. How? They will use apps to check their health. This will help a lot of people. Lastly, there will be new jobs. Think about the future when we can travel to space. Then there will be space tour guides! Thinking about the future is fun. But here is the key: We can guess the future. Still, no one knows the future for sure.

New Words

pill

n a small piece of medicine

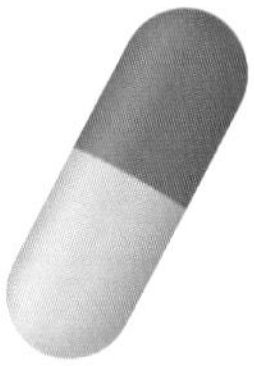

vacation

n a long break from work or school

technology

n modern machines

expert

n

ex Does she know a lot about cars? Then she is an expert on cars.

insect

n a bug

cancer

n a very serious disease

Part A. Sentence Completion

1. _______ one knows the teacher very well.

(A) No
(B) Not
(C) None
(D) Nothing

2. The candies in the box _______ for Ms. Stein.

(A) is
(B) are
(C) to be
(D) being

Part B. Situational Writing

3.

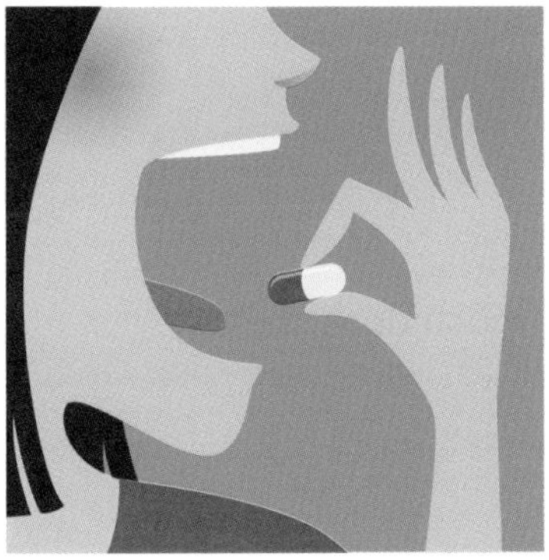

Jisu _______ every day.

(A) takes a pill
(B) drinks juice
(C) sells medicine
(D) goes to the doctor

4.

The food on the right is _______ than the food on the left.

(A) green
(B) greener
(C) unhealthy
(D) less healthy

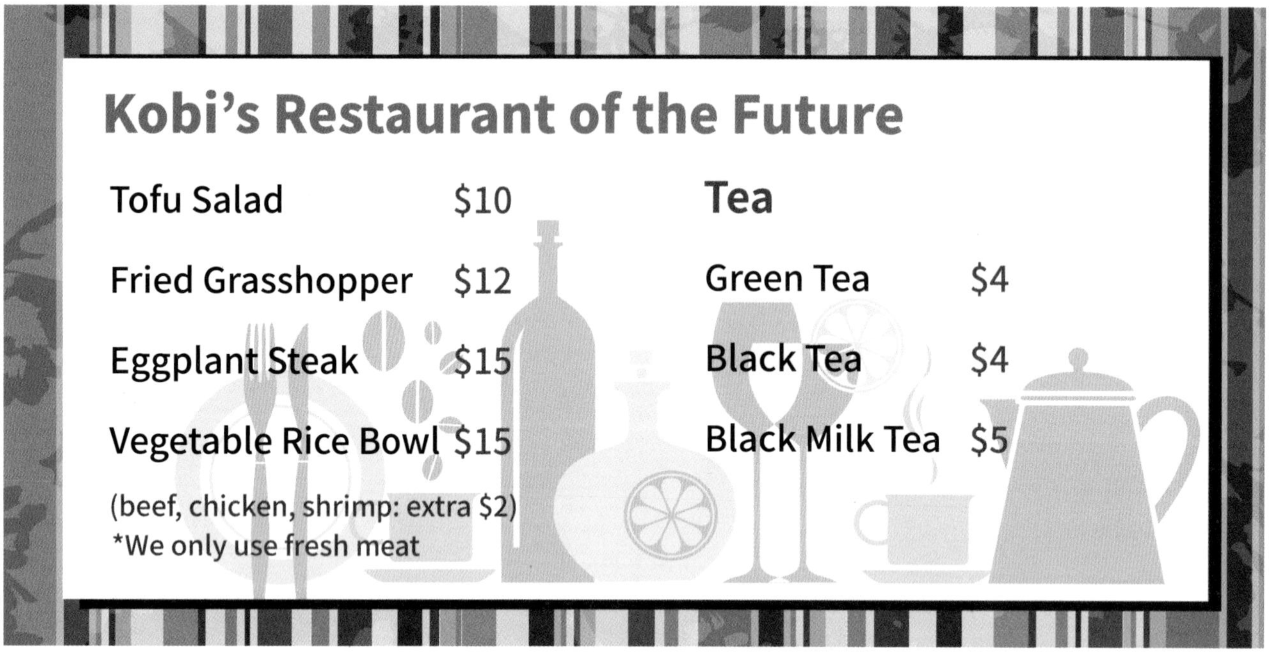

5. How much is a vegetable rice bowl with chicken?

   (A) $13
   (B) $15
   (C) $17
   (D) $19

6. Donna orders a bowl of tofu salad and a cup of black tea. How much does she pay?

   (A) $10
   (B) $14
   (C) $16
   (D) $20

Part D. General Reading and Retelling

What will life be like in 2035? How will it be different? Will there be flying cars, food pills, or a vacation on Mars? Is it going to be like a movie? Sadly, technology may not be that great. It may be less exciting. Technology expert Dean Evans tells you all about it! First, he talks about food. The future of food is ________ than today. People will be eating more vegetables and less meat. That's because people will start to eat healthier. People will eat more insects, too. In parts of Asia, people are already eating insects. That's because insects are low in fat. What about the future of health? Will doctors cure everyone who has cancer? No, but there is good news! People will be able to check their health at home. How? They will use apps to check their health. This will help a lot of people. Lastly, there will be new jobs. Think about the future when we can travel to space. Then there will be space tour guides! Thinking about the future is fun. But here is the key: We can guess the future. Still, no one knows the future for sure.

7. What is the best title for the passage?

   (A) Insects Are Full of Fat
   (B) Life Changes in 2035
   (C) New Jobs Will Kill Other Jobs
   (D) People Are Becoming Healthier

8. Who is Dean Evans?

   (A) a cook
   (B) a doctor
   (C) a tour guide
   (D) a technology expert

9. Which word goes best in the blank?

   (A) oilier
   (B) heavier
   (C) sweeter
   (D) greener

10. What is mentioned about our life in 2035?

    (A) Cars will fly to space.
    (B) People will eat more meat.
    (C) Insects will no longer be food.
    (D) People will check their health at home.

Listening Practice

Listen and write.

MP3 B3-12

How Will 2035 Be Different?

What will life be like in 2035? How will it be different? Will there be flying cars, food [1] ______________, or a [2] ______________ on Mars? Is it going to be like a movie? Sadly, [3] ______________ may not be that great. It may be less exciting. Technology [4] ______________ Dean Evans tells you all about it! First, he talks about food. The future of food is greener than today. People will be eating more vegetables and less meat. That's because people will start to eat healthier. People will eat more [5] ______________, too. In parts of Asia, people are already eating insects. That's because insects are low in fat. What about the future of health? Will doctors cure everyone who has [6] ______________? No, but there is good news! People will be able to check their health at home. How? They will use apps to check their health. This will help a lot of people. Lastly, there will be new jobs. Think about the future when we can travel to space. Then there will be space tour guides! Thinking about the future is fun. But here is the key: We can guess the future. Still, no one knows the future for sure.

Word Bank

technology	vacation	pills
expirt	fills	canser
cancer	expert	vacattion
teknology	insecks	insects

Listen. Pause. Say each sentence.

MP3 B3-12G

Writing Practice

Write the words.

1 ____________

n a small piece of medicine

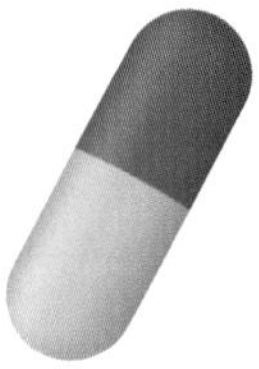

2 ____________

n a long break from work or school

3 ____________

n modern machines

4 ____________

n

ex Does she know a lot about cars? Then she is an ______ on cars.

5 ____________

n a bug

6 ____________

n a very serious disease

Write the words in each blank.

Summary

Dean Evans talks about year 2035. Maybe in the ______________, people will eat more vegetables and ______________. Second, people will ______________ their health with apps. And maybe there ______________ be new jobs.

Word Puzzle

Complete the word puzzle.

2↓
a very serious disease

1→
a bug

6↓
modern machines

3→
a long break from work or school

4→
Does she know a lot about cars? Then she is an _______ on cars.

5↓
a small piece of medicine

CHAPTER REVIEW

What Is It?

Teacher's Book p.213

Person A: Read Questions 1 to 11.
Person B: Read the answers.
Then, try to guess together. Who or what is it?

	Questions	Answers
1	Is it an artist?	No, it is not a person.
2	Is it a sea turtle?	No, it's not an animal.
3	Is it a desert?	No, it's not a place.
4	Is it a carrot?	No, it's not a vegetable.
5	Is it a pair of sunglasses?	No, but it is an object.
6	Is this object bigger than a suitcase?	No, it's smaller than a suitcase.
7	Can a person carry it?	Yes, a person can carry it.
8	Is it made of glass?	No, it's not.
9	Can you put something in it?	Yes, you can put hot or cold drinks in it.
10	Can you wash it?	No, you can't.
11	Is it good for the earth?	No, not really.

ANSWERS

CHAPTER 1 | Travel
p.10

UNIT 1 B3-1 p.11

1 (A) 2 (C) 3 (D) 4 (D) 5 (A) 6 (C) 7 (B) 8 (A) 9 (C) 10 (C)
1 sand 2 Sunset 3 Sunrise 4 friendly 5 visitors 6 fee
1 sand 2 sunrise 3 sunset 4 friendly 5 visitor 6 fee
island, sand beaches, fire, hotels
→ 2 fee 3 visitor 4 sunset ↓ 1 sunrise 2 friendly 4 sand

UNIT 2 B3-2 p.19

1 (B) 2 (D) 3 (C) 4 (C) 5 (C) 6 (B) 7 (C) 8 (C) 9 (C) 10 (C)
1 lost 2 all about 3 international 4 suitcases 5 baggage 6 claim
1 get lost 2 all about 3 international flight 4 suitcase 5 baggage 6 baggage claim area
London, grandparents, airport, mother
→ 4 baggage claim area ↓ 1 suitcase 2 international flight 3 all about 4 baggage 5 get lost

UNIT 3 B3-3 p.27

1 (D) 2 (A) 3 (D) 4 (B) 5 (A) 6 (C) 7 (B) 8 (A) 9 (C) 10 (B)
1 offices 2 towers 3 design 4 safety 5 thousand 6 That's
1 office 2 design 3 twin towers 4 thousand 5 safety 6 that's why
buildings, twin, design, bridge
→ 5 twin towers ↓ 1 thousand 2 safety 3 that's why 4 design 6 office

UNIT 4 B3-4 p.35

1 (C) 2 (B) 3 (A) 4 (B) 5 (D) 6 (C) 7 (C) 8 (D) 9 (D) 10 (A)
1 mistakes 2 travel 3 manners 4 history 5 Copying 6 allow
1 travel 2 make a mistake 3 manners 4 history 5 allow 6 copy
manners, read, follow, pictures
→ 2 make a mistake 3 travel 4 manners 6 copy ↓ 1 history 5 allow

CHAPTER 2 | Culture
p.44

UNIT 5 B3-5 p.45

1 (B) 2 (D) 3 (B) 4 (C) 5 (A) 6 (B) 7 (B) 8 (B) 9 (B) 10 (A)
1 adults 2 turkey 3 vegetarian 4 close 5 dining 6 parade
1 adult 2 turkey 3 vegetarian 4 We are close 5 dining room 6 parade
grandparents, ten, eat, vegetarians
→ 2 adult 5 parade 6 turkey ↓ 1 we are close 3 dining room 4 vegetarian

UNIT 6 B3-6 p.53

1 (B) 2 (C) 3 (A) 4 (C) 5 (D) 6 (A) 7 (D) 8 (D) 9 (B) 10 (B)
1 went to bed 2 take a nap 3 break 4 continued 5 cool 6 These days
1 go to bed late 2 break 3 take a nap 4 continue with your story 5 cool 6 these days
break, hot, restaurants, these days
→ 1 cool 4 go to bed late ↓ 1 continue with your story 2 break 3 take a nap 5 these days

UNIT 7 B3-7 p.61

1 (A) 2 (C) 3 (A) 4 (B) 5 (D) 6 (A) 7 (A) 8 (A) 9 (B) 10 (C)
1 tidy 2 Modern 3 tomb 4 treasures 5 ill 6 weak
1 tidy 2 tomb 3 modern 4 treasure 5 ill 6 weak
Egypt, learn, tomb, died
→ 1 tomb 2 weak 3 modern 4 tidy ↓ 1 treasure 5 ill

UNIT 8 B3-8 p.69

1 (A) 2 (C) 3 (D) 4 (A) 5 (C) 6 (B) 7 (C) 8 (C) 9 (D) 10 (B)
1 wide 2 stripe 3 cactus 4 capital 5 similar 6 soldier
1 wide 2 stripe 3 cactus 4 capital 5 similar 6 soldier
flag, Mexican, white, snake
→ 4 wide 5 capital 6 soldier ↓ 1 stripe 2 similar 3 cactus

CHAPTER 3 | Nature & the Earth
p.78

UNIT 9 B3-9 p.79

1 (C) 2 (A) 3 (D) 4 (D) 5 (A) 6 (C) 7 (D) 8 (C) 9 (D) 10 (D)
1 interested in 2 habitat 3 scientist 4 need 5 space 6 Sharks
1 habitat 2 be interested in 3 scientist 4 need 5 space 6 shark
habitat, plants, air, food
→ 3 scientist 4 shark 5 need ↓ 1 be interested in 2 habitat 4 space

UNIT 10 B3-10 p.87

1 (D) 2 (C) 3 (A) 4 (B) 5 (B) 6 (B) 7 (D) 8 (C) 9 (C) 10 (B)
1 global 2 melting 3 desert 4 bigger 5 humans 6 lakes
1 global warming 2 melt 3 human 4 desert 5 get bigger 6 lake
bigger, two, warming, water
→ 3 get bigger 4 lake 5 human ↓ 1 melt 2 desert 3 global warming

UNIT 11 B3-11 p.95

1 (C) 2 (D) 3 (C) 4 (C) 5 (C) 6 (A) 7 (A) 8 (A) 9 (D) 10 (A)
1 turn off 2 brush 3 glasses 4 print 5 leave 6 parent
1 brush your teeth 2 turn off 3 print 4 glass 5 leave 6 parent
earth, brush, turn off, leave
→ 2 turn off 3 glass 4 print 5 leave ↓ 1 brush your teeth 4 parent

UNIT 12 B3-12 p.103

1 (A) 2 (B) 3 (A) 4 (B) 5 (C) 6 (B) 7 (B) 8 (D) 9 (D) 10 (D)
1 pills 2 vacation 3 technology 4 expert 5 insects 6 cancer
1 pill 2 vacation 3 technology 4 expert 5 insect 6 cancer
future, insects, check, will
→ 1 insect 3 vacation 4 expert ↓ 2 cancer 5 pill 6 technology